CONTENTS

CONTENTS

Shocking Electricity

CA 9/12

HORRIBLE SCIENCE

KILLER ENERGY

2 Books in 1

SHOCKING ELECTRICITY

NICK ARNOLD   illustrated by **TONY DE SAULLES**

■SCHOLASTIC

www.horrible-science.co.uk

www.nickarnold-website.com
www.tonydesaulles.co.uk

Scholastic Children's Books,
Euston House, 24 Eversholt Street,
London, NW1 1DB, UK

A division of Scholastic Ltd
London ~ New York ~ Toronto ~ Sydney ~ Auckland
Mexico City ~ New Delhi ~ Hong Kong

First published in the UK in this edition by Scholastic Ltd, 2006
This edition published 2009

Killer Energy
First published in the UK by Scholastic Ltd, 2001
Text copyright © Nick Arnold, 2001
Illustrations © Tony De Saulles, 2001

Shocking Electricity
First published in the UK by Scholastic Ltd, 2000
Text copyright © Nick Arnold, 2000
Illustrations © Tony De Saulles, 2000

All rights reserved

ISBN 978 1407 10997 8

Page layout services provided by Quadrum Solutions Ltd, Mumbai, India
Printed and bound in the UK by CPI Bookmarque, Croydon

2 4 6 8 10 9 7 5 3 1

The right of Nick Arnold and Tony De Saulles to be identified as the author and
illustrator of this work respectively has been asserted by them in accordance
with the Copyright, Designs and Patents Act, 1988.

This book is sold subject to the condition that it shall not, by way of trade or
otherwise be lent, resold, hired out, or otherwise circulated without the
publisher's prior consent in any form of binding or cover other than that in
which it is published and without a similar condition, including this condition,
being imposed on a subsequent purchaser.

KILLER ENERGY

INTRODUCTION

I hope you're not easily scared, because … you're about to meet a huge, horribly powerful MONSTER!

It's a very, very old monster (yes, it's even older than your science teacher). In fact, it's so incredibly ancient that it's as old as time itself. And the amazing thing about this monster is that it's always around but no one has ever seen it – *well not until now that is*!

The monster's name is ENERGY…

The Energy Monster gets everywhere. It makes stars shine and bonfires burn, and it moves everything from the slowest slug to the speediest spacecraft. But don't go thinking that the Energy Monster is a helpful gentle giant. No way! Take a deep breath and read on … if you dare!

Sometimes the Energy Monster is a cruel, crazed, KILLER that destroys humans in hundreds of horrible ways. Of course, ordinary science books don't dwell on these disgusting details but this is a *Horrible Science* book – and that means you can read the killer energy info you *really* want to know, such as…

• Why this lucky man is bursting into flames because of a fart…

• Why this man is eating greasy fat for breakfast…

• And why this scientist is getting rats drunk…

• Plus, the ULTIMATE FATE OF THE UNIVERSE (and whether it'll spoil your holiday this year).

HORRIBLE HEALTH WARNING!

This book contains foul facts, rude words and blood-thirsty cartoons. This material may shock teachers and other sensitive persons.

SHOCK! HORROR!

Hopefully, though, you're made of sterner stuff. Now, have you got enough energy to turn the page?

ER...WELL, OK THEN

THE ULTIMATE POWER

Is your brain powered up? Well, this killer question will get it going so fast that steam could blast out of your ears. Ready? OK, here it is…

What do the following have in common?

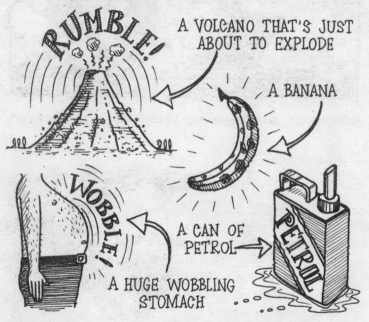

RUMBLE!

A VOLCANO THAT'S JUST ABOUT TO EXPLODE

A BANANA

WOBBLE!

A CAN OF PETROL →

PETROL

A HUGE WOBBLING STOMACH

Give up?

Well, they all store *energy*…

The volcano stores movement energy. And when the volcano explodes you'll need lots of movement energy to run away. Bananas are great energy stores which is why some tennis players eat at least six every match. Petrol is a fuel so it's "fuel" of energy, and the bulging belly contains fat which is yet another food energy store…

Now at this point we were going to ask a teacher to tell us what energy is. But we couldn't find one who knew ... see what I mean?

Honestly ... do I have to explain *everything* round here?

Killer energy fact file

NAME: Energy

THE BASIC FACTS: 1 Energy is the power that gets things moving. Since everything in the universe is moving, everything in the universe is powered by energy.

IT'S ALL GREEK TO ME!

2 The word "energy" isn't too helpful – it just means "activity" in Greek.

3 Energy takes many forms...

COAL

• Stored energy in fuel and food and other chemicals.

ENERGY STORED IN HERE

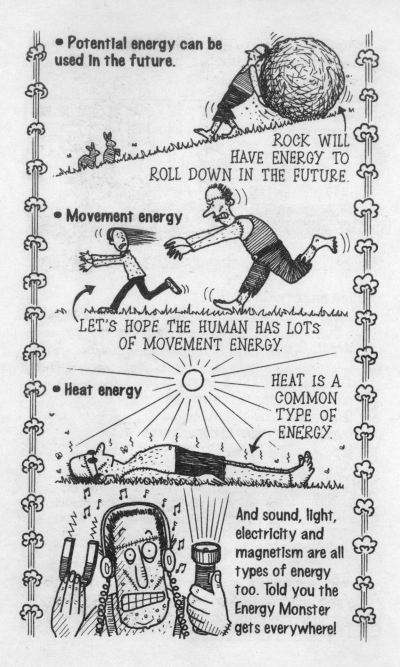

- Potential energy can be used in the future.

ROCK WILL HAVE ENERGY TO ROLL DOWN IN THE FUTURE.

- Movement energy

LET'S HOPE THE HUMAN HAS LOTS OF MOVEMENT ENERGY.

- Heat energy

HEAT IS A COMMON TYPE OF ENERGY.

And sound, light, electricity and magnetism are all types of energy too. Told you the Energy Monster gets everywhere!

KILLER DETAILS: Every execution method uses energy in one form or another. As you can see...

KILLER BLADE HAS POTENTIAL ENERGY TO FALL AT ANY SECOND

With me so far?

So energy gets things moving and takes different forms. But someone had to figure this out. As you can imagine, scientists in the past had some really wrong ideas about energy. Here are four scientists to argue their points of view...

THE GREAT ENERGY DEBATE

Famous Greek philosopher, **Aristotle** (384–322 BC)

Not-so-famous Greek philosopher, **Anaxagoras** (500–428 BC)

German scientist, philosopher, mathematician, historian and all-round know-all, **Gottfried Leibniz** (1646–1716)

German scientist, **Georg Ernst Stahl** (1660–1734)

14

These ideas were as sensible as attacking a lion's mane with a razor, running five miles to escape, and then shouting: "HOW'S THAT FOR A CLOSE SHAVE!"

It took scientists until the 1850s for a number of them (working separately) to begin to make scientific sense of energy. And then they came up with the Laws of Thermodynamics (that's ther-mo-dy-nam-ics). And if you thought I said "thermal underwear" you really need to read the next chapter to find out what the heck I'm going on about…

LAYING DOWN THE LAWS

In this chapter you'll find out about the Laws of Thermodynamics. They sound dead posh and impressive but actually they're horribly easy to understand. (Don't tell anyone how easy, and with luck your friends will think you are a scientific genius!)

Killer energy fact file

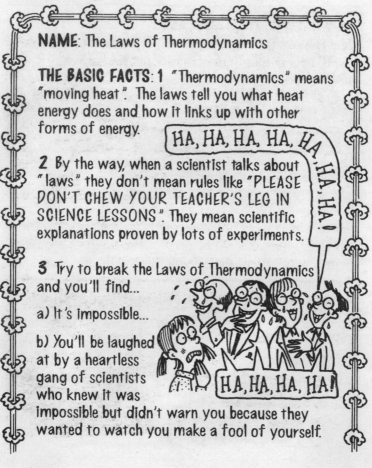

NAME: The Laws of Thermodynamics

THE BASIC FACTS: **1** "Thermodynamics" means "moving heat". The laws tell you what heat energy does and how it links up with other forms of energy.

HA, HA, HA, HA, HA, HA, HA!

2 By the way, when a scientist talks about "laws" they don't mean rules like "PLEASE DON'T CHEW YOUR TEACHER'S LEG IN SCIENCE LESSONS". They mean scientific explanations proven by lots of experiments.

3 Try to break the Laws of Thermodynamics and you'll find...

a) It's impossible...

b) You'll be laughed at by a heartless gang of scientists who knew it was impossible but didn't warn you because they wanted to watch you make a fool of yourself.

HA, HA, HA, HA!

KILLER DETAILS: The search for these laws drove one scientist into madness. → Let's hope you're more fortunate...

THERMO DIE MANIC! DON'T PANIC! RAVE! JIBBER!

SO, WHAT DO THE LAWS SAY?

Meet Harvey Tucker, the BIGGEST journalist in Australia – well, he's certainly the largest (and the laziest).

G'DAY SPORTS!

Later on he'll be investigating energy (that's if he can be bothered). But for now, we've managed to persuade Harvey to report on how the Laws work...

THE LAWS OF THERMODYNAMICS

Well, I wasn't too hot on thermo ... heat energy, but no worries – I surfed stacks of info from the Internet.

17

Phew — it's hard yakka! Anyway, here's the low-down...

LAW ONE

Energy can't be made or destroyed. But heat energy can be used to power movement energy and movement energy can turn into heat energy. Streuth! That's fair dinkums. If I did some work I'd have more movement energy and this would make me feel more heat energy. So I'd best sit here with my lager and save my energy — BURP!

HEAT ENERGY → POWERS → MOVEMENT ENERGY

HEAT ENERGY ← CAN TURN INTO ← MOVEMENT ENERGY

LAW TWO

Heat energy always moves from hot things to cold things. So heat from the sun is warming up my cold lager. Well, talk about stating the blithering obvious! If heat went from cold places to hot places my lager would *cool down* in the sun — well, that *would* be the day! I'm fair cooked already!

HOT SUN

HEAT ALWAYS MOVES IN THIS DIRECTION

COLD BEER

LAW THREE

You can't get colder than -273.16°C (-459.67°F) - otherwise known as **ABSOLUTE ZERO**. The scientists say when something's this cold it ain't got no heat energy! Lucky it doesn't get that cold in Oz - I do feel the cold, see?

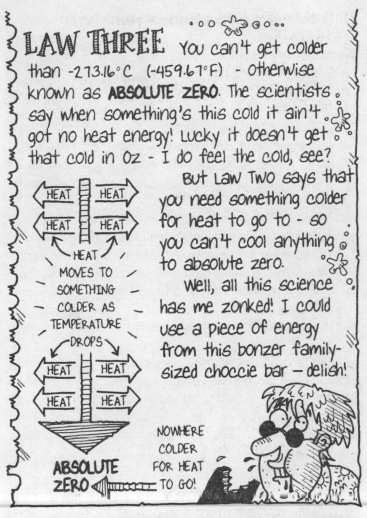

HEAT → HEAT →
← HEAT ← HEAT
↑ HEAT ↗
MOVES TO
SOMETHING
COLDER AS
TEMPERATURE
↙ DROPS ↘
← HEAT HEAT →
← HEAT HEAT

ABSOLUTE ZERO

NOWHERE COLDER FOR HEAT TO GO!

But Law Two says that you need something colder for heat to go to - so you can't cool anything to absolute zero.

Well, all this science has me zonked! I could use a piece of energy from this bonzer family-sized choccie bar – delish!

We'll be taking a look at Laws Two and Three in the next two chapters, but for now we'll stick to Law One. Did you know that a scientist who worked on the first law got his ideas from *blood*? Yes, it's true!

Read on for the bloodthirsty details...

Hall of Fame: Julius Robert von Mayer
(1814–1878)
Nationality: German

"Ach mein Gott – I hev cut an artery! Hold still or you vill bleed to death!"

As he spoke the young doctor turned white and his hands began to shake as he held the bowl to the sailor's brawny arm. The bowl was steadily filling with blood. Bright red, glistening blood, the kind that squirts from the heart through the high-pressure arteries.

But the sailor's face crinkled into a weak smile. It was a painful smile because the blood was still draining from his arm and he was exhausted from fever.

"Don't you fret, doc – our blood always comes out this red in these parts. I don't understand it, mind, but there it is."

With his mind racing, the doctor set down the bowl of blood. Then he bandaged the crewman's arm with a grubby strip of material to staunch the blood that was still trickling from his arm.

In 1840 doctors like Mayer believed the best way to treat disease was to drain blood from their patients' veins. But when Julius tried to do this in Java he found the blood was bright red, even in veins where it's usually dark red. Julius Mayer was about to make a great discovery.

It nearly destroyed him.

Julius was not a lucky person. He didn't do well at school and he was expelled from university for joining a secret club that was frowned on by his teachers. (Today's teachers are a bit more understanding, so you may escape being expelled for joining the Horrible Club.)

Mayer was allowed back into university the following year. He studied medicine and became a ship's doctor – and that's how he came to be in Java in 1840. Seeing the red blood got him thinking. Here's how Mayer might have made sense of the puzzle in letters to his best friend – his brother…

Jakarta, Java 1841

Dear Fritz,

Remember the red blood I mentioned in my last letter? I do, I can't stop thinking about it, and now I've got an idea!

1. Bright red blood contains oxygen. The body needs oxygen in order to live – that's why we breathe! ⟶

2. The blood in the sailor's veins was bright red with oxygen. Since veins carry blood back from the body this means the sailor's body is using less oxygen than usual.

OXYGEN

3. I think the body uses oxygen to keep warm. But when it's hot (like here — sorry about the sweat stains!) the body needs less heat so it uses less oxygen. Yes, I think I've cracked it! What do you think?

Your bruv,

Jools

MORE OXYGEN

LESS OXYGEN

Jakarta, Java 1841

Hi Fritz,

It's me again...

Don't know what's got into me — but I've suddenly had loads of WONDERFUL NEW IDEAS!

1. I think the body needs food as well as oxygen to make heat. It's a bit like a fire that needs fuel and oxygen to burn properly.

FOOD + OXYGEN

2. This means energy must switch from one form to another. Yes, I reckon energy must be stored in food and turn into heat and movement energy inside the body.

Am I *hot* on the
trail – or is my
brain over-heating?
I can't wait to
get home and tell
everyone!
Your very excited bruv,
Jools

Mayer was right not once but TWICE!! He'd made not one but TWO brilliant breakthroughs! He'd figured how the body uses energy *and* he'd got the idea for the First Law of Thermodynamics. (Remember, it showed the link between heat and movement energy.) Of course, all the other scientists were thrilled and Jools became famous and lived happily ever after ... didn't he?

HOORAY!

NO!

Excuse me – this is *Horrible Science* not some sloppy-soppy little fairy tale! Mayer wrote an article and sent it to a science magazine but they didn't reply. No one believed him because he hadn't done any experiments to prove his ideas. So Mayer studied science for months and months until he knew enough to re-write the article in more scientific language. But by the time the article was published other scientists had put forward the same idea.

There were heated rows over who'd thought of the First Law first…

Bet you never knew!

1 One of the rival scientists was a Briton, James Joule (1818–1889). James's family was so rich he never had to go to school (he even had a top scientist, John Dalton (1766–1844), as his very own personal teacher).

AND I'D LIKE THE NEXT THREE WEEKS OFF, DALTON!

YES, CERTAINLY MASTER JAMES

(You could ask your parents to let you off school and pay for your own teacher, and if you happen to be dreaming they might even say "YES!")

2 James had a private lab for energy experiments. In 1843 he found out, by measuring the temperature of water turned by a paddle, that movement energy can be turned into heat energy.

3 Today, scientists measure energy in joules. One joule gives you enough energy to lift an apple one metre – can you do this?

GO ON!

UUUUGH!

YOU CAN DO IT!

Now back to miserable Mayer…

Julius Mayer's luck hadn't turned. He fell in love and got married but five of his seven children died of disease. Revolution broke out in Germany, and Fritz supported the revolution, but Julius was arrested for opposing it. He was soon released but fell out with his brother. Julius grew increasingly miserable about his lack of scientific success. One unhappy day, he decided to take his own life. He failed but his family thought he was mad and he spent ten years locked in mental hospitals.

I'VE JUST DISCOVERED THE FOURTH LAW OF THERMODYNAMICS – **DON'T TELL ANYBODY ABOUT THE FIRST THREE!**

It was only years later that scientists came to realize that the First Law of Thermodynamics was correct. At last, when Mayer was a broken old man, the Royal Society, Britain's top science club, gave him a gold medal. But talking about the First Law – here's an experiment that shows it in action. Go on, give it a go – it's easy!

Dare you discover ... the First Law of Thermodynamics?
You will need:

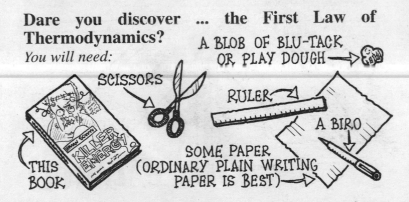

A BLOB OF BLU-TACK OR PLAY DOUGH→

SCISSORS

RULER

A BIRO

THIS BOOK

SOME PAPER (ORDINARY PLAIN WRITING PAPER IS BEST)→

What you do:

1 Place the paper over this shape and trace round it. Draw in the fold line using the ruler.

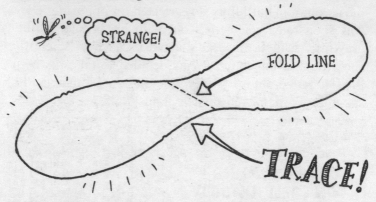

2 Cut out the shape you've drawn. DON'T cut out the shape from your *Horrible Science* book, *especially* if it comes from the library! Fold one side of the shape along the line. Unfold the shape.

3 Stick the blu-tack on a table and stick the pen in it, so it's standing on end. Make sure the pen is upright (use the ruler to check).

4 Turn the shape upside down and balance it on the point of the biro so that the sides point downwards at about 45° – carefully does it!

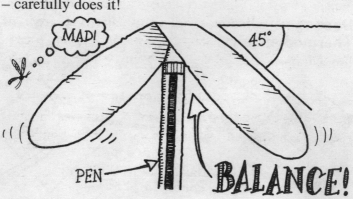

5 Watch what happens to the shape for a minute or two. Then place your hands on their sides on the table to make a circle round the biro. (If your hands are cold you need to rub them until they're warm.)

What do you notice?
a) The shape rocks backwards and forwards.
b) The shape whizzes into the air.
c) The shape moves around and then stops. When I put my hands near it the shape moves round faster than before.

Answer:
c) The shape is powered by heat energy! It might move at first because of draughts in the room or wobble as it balances on top of the pen. But it really gets going when the hot air rises off your hands. This proves the First Law is right when it says that heat energy can make things move.

But talking about heat – it just so happens that the next chapter is all about this cosy topic … will you warm to it?

HORRIBLE HEAT

This chapter lets you into some sizzling heat secrets, including how the Second Law affects the entire universe and how an extremely important sausage changed the course of history...

What's that? You don't remember what the Second Law says? Well, it's the one that says heat energy goes from a hot object to a cooler area. And actually, come to think of it, the Second Law actually sneaked into that experiment in the last chapter.

IN THE EXPERIMENT HEAT ENERGY PASSED FROM A HOT AREA — YOUR HOT, STICKY HANDS — TO A COOLER AREA — THE AIR.

YIKES!

And as I said, the Second Law has a HUGE effect on the whole universe. Take this nice hot cup of tea...

HOT!

IS MY TEA READY YET?

The Second Law says all the time the cup of tea is losing heat energy. In other words, it's cooling down. If you blow on the tea, it will cool even faster.

Your breath blows away the air warmed by the hot tea and the heat energy flows more quickly into the cooler air.

BLOW!

> ## SCIENTIFIC NOTE
>
> The greater the temperature difference between a hot and a cold area the faster the heat will flow between them.

In half an hour the tea is disgustingly lukewarm.

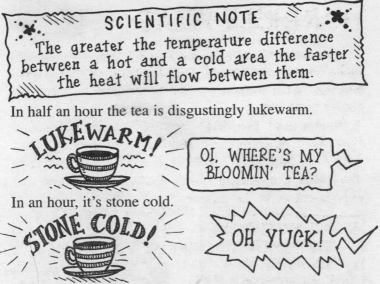

In an hour, it's stone cold.

The only way to make the tea hot is to heat it up again – in other words to add more heat energy!

And what's true for the tea is also true for everything in the *entire universe*. Yes, the Second Law says that *everything*, from galaxies to gravy, from hippos to hotwater bottles, is forever cooling down. Your body is losing heat and so is an alien starship on the other side of the cosmos.

*WE'RE LOSING HEAT, CAPTAIN!

*IT'S THAT BLASTED 2ND LAW, AGAIN!

And the only way to keep anything hot is to chuck in more heat energy. And that means you'd better eat your dad's revolting rice pudding and digest it and turn it into heat to replace the heat energy you lost today.

And that rotten old Second Law has some even worse news for you on page 143. But first it's time to find out a bit more about a real hot topic…

Killer energy fact file

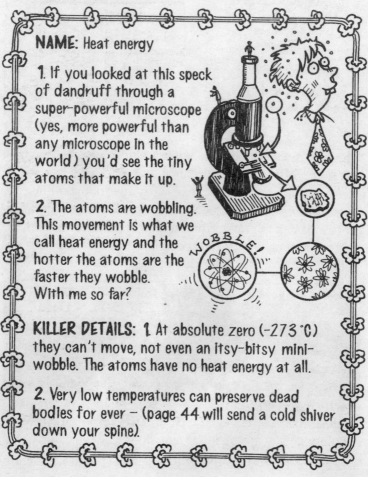

NAME: Heat energy

1. If you looked at this speck of dandruff through a super-powerful microscope (yes, more powerful than any microscope in the world) you'd see the tiny atoms that make it up.

2. The atoms are wobbling. This movement is what we call heat energy and the hotter the atoms are the faster they wobble. With me so far?

WOBBLE!

KILLER DETAILS: 1. At absolute zero (−273 °C) they can't move, not even an itsy-bitsy mini-wobble. The atoms have no heat energy at all.

2. Very low temperatures can preserve dead bodies for ever − (page 44 will send a cold shiver down your spine).

NOT SO HOT THEORIES...

You can't expect scientists to grasp all this straight away and early ideas about heat were definitely on the tepid side. Here's Swiss scientist Pierre Prévost (1751–1839).

Some people think that hot and cold are invisible substances — they call the cold substance "frigoric".

PIFFLE! It's obvious that cold is simply lack of heat...

Oh yes, and the hot substance is called "caloric"

Of course this "caloric" was a load of hot air, but Prévost wasn't proved wrong until American scientist Benjamin Thompson, Count Rumford (1753–814), took on a boring job. He worked as Minister for War in Bavaria, Germany, and he was watching a cannon being bored by a drill. The cannon got very hot and, if you believed in caloric, you might think that the cannon would run out of the hot stuff after a while. But it didn't!

So Rumford realized that heat can't be a substance – it must be a form of energy that was picked up from the rubbing of the drill in the same way that rubbing your hands makes them feel warmer. In 1798 Rumford proudly announced his discovery at a meeting of the Royal Society and ... no one took any notice.

They must have been bored...

TERRIBLY TACKY THERMOMETERS

The measurement of heat energy is called temperature (I hope you're suitably impressed by this fact). But early scientists had a problem measuring heat as no one had got around to inventing the thermometer. After combing dozens of scientific junk shops we've uncovered a selection of ancient thermometers...

Ye Olde Scientific Junk Shop

SALE TODAY

LET'S HOPE YOUR SCHOOL EQUIPMENT ISN'T THIS OLD — EVEN IF YOUR SCIENCE TEACHER MIGHT BE.

Air-filled thermoscope invented by Italian genius Galileo Galilei (1564 – 1642) – uses air and water to measure temperature.

Albert Einstein's eyeballs

Galileo's skull

Improved version devised by German scientist Otto von Guericke (1602-1686).

Isaac Newton's wig and teeth

Water-filled thermometer invented by French doctor Jean Rey in 1631. It wasn't much good at measuring below freezing – can anyone think why?

Some of the earliest mercury thermometers were made by German Daniel Fahrenheit (1686-1736) in 1714. Mercury freezes at a very low temperature and boils at a very high temperature.

Albert Einstein's brain

Dare you discover . . . how to make your own thermoscope?

You will need:

STICKY TAPE   TEASPOON   SCISSORS

A SMALL PLASTIC BOTTLE (IDEALLY NO MORE THAN 30 ML WITH AS SMALL AN OPENING AS POSSIBLE)

A LARGE BLOB OF BLU-TACK   THREE GLASSES

FOOD COLOURING → FC

A LIGHT-COLOURED PLASTIC DRINKING STRAW

What you do:

1 Half-fill one glass with water and add a few drops of food colouring. Stir well.

2 Half-fill the second glass with ice from the freezer (be careful not to touch the ice with your bare hands).

3 Half-fill the third glass with hot water from the tap. (Don't touch the water either – it could be scalding!)

4 Stick the straw in the bottle and block up the rest of the opening with blu-tack. Wrap sticky tape round the blu-tack so no air can get into the bottle except through the straw.

DRIP!   CHILL!

SCALD!

AIRTIGHT →

5 Gently squeeze the bottle and turn it upside-down so the end of the straw is in the coloured water. Coloured water will flow up the straw. Now stop squeezing the bottle and put it the right way up. You should see a band of coloured water in the straw.

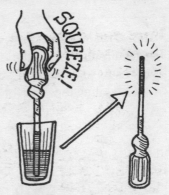

6 Place the bottle in the glass of ice and then in the hot water.

What do you notice?
a) The water in the straw goes up in the ice and down in the hot water.
b) The water in the straw goes up in the hot water and down in the ice.
c) The water in the straw becomes lighter in the ice and darker in the hot water.

Answer:
b) Remember those wobbling atoms on page 30? When you heat up the air in the bottle, the atoms have energy and try to move off in all directions – think of a class of energetic kids running outside at break-time.

The warm air atoms push up the straw and they push the water up too. When the air is cold the atoms have less heat energy so they don't want to go anywhere – think of kids huddling together for warmth on a cold day.

The pressure of the air pushing down on the straw from above pushes the water level down.

Bet you never knew!
The plans of Galileo's thermoscope were amongst his papers when the great man died. Galileo left his papers to scientist, Vincenzo Viviani (1622–1703). But when Viviani died, his family thought the papers were worthless rubbish, so they sold them to a local sausage maker to wrap his bangers. Then another scientist ate one of the sausages and read the writing on the wrapper. He bought the entire stock of wrappers including the designs for the thermoscope. And so it was that Galileo's great discoveries were saved – thanks to a sausage.

36

TRICKY TEMPERATURE FACTS

1 Scientists still had a problem. They had thermometers but they couldn't agree on a scale to measure temperature. Scientists made up their own measurements – and this no doubt led to heated arguments.

2 The first widely used measure of temperature was invented by our pal Daniel Fahrenheit – can you guess what it was called?

3 Fahrenheit decided that the coldest temperature he could make by mixing chemicals in his lab was 0°. This meant that water froze at 32° and the temperature of the human body was 96° (that's three times 32°). But Fahrenheit hadn't got it right – the body is around 98.6° so his carefully planned scale was wrong.

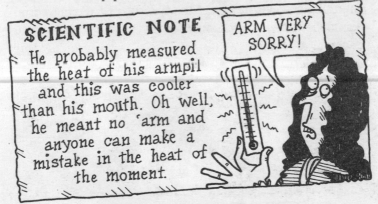

4 Fahrenheit's scale is now used in the USA but the rest of the world uses a measurement invented by a Swedish scientist named Anders Celsius (1701–1744). It's sometimes called centigrade but the official name is the Celsius scale after its inventor.

Anders was the son of a Professor of Astronomy and he grew up interested in maths and science. He loved exploring and went on two trips to the north of Finland. There he studied the northern lights and made observations that proved the Earth was slightly flattened at the North Pole.

5 Anders suggested a scale of 100° with water boiling at 0° and ice melting at 100°. Yes, you did read that right – Anders Celsius put his scale the wrong way round but another scientist reversed it after his death. Oh well, I guess they had a "measured" approach to science.

But talking about freezing, there's lots of freezing going on in the next chapter. In fact the next chapter's cold enough to freeze a cup of tea rock-hard *in one millisecond*!

Are you wrapped up *really* warm?

THE DEAD FREEZING CHAPTER

If science leaves you cold you might be gob-smacked to hear that science really can be cool – in fact *supercool*! Yes, this chapter and the next one are about losing heat energy and the science of low temperatures.

THE BIG FREEZE-UP

Remember the Third Law of Thermodynamics – the one that says that you can't get colder than absolute zero? (See page 19 if you don't.) Bet you never knew that one scientist who worked on this law went to university when he was just *ten years old*. He's been dead for ages but we've zapped him with energy for one last interview…

Dead Brainy: William Thomson, Lord Kelvin (1824–1907)

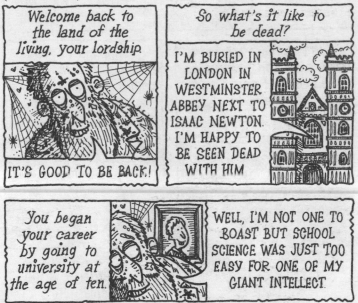

Welcome back to the land of the living, your lordship.

IT'S GOOD TO BE BACK!

So what's it like to be dead?

I'M BURIED IN LONDON IN WESTMINSTER ABBEY NEXT TO ISAAC NEWTON. I'M HAPPY TO BE SEEN DEAD WITH HIM

You began your career by going to university at the age of ten.

WELL, I'M NOT ONE TO BOAST BUT SCHOOL SCIENCE WAS JUST TOO EASY FOR ONE OF MY GIANT INTELLECT.

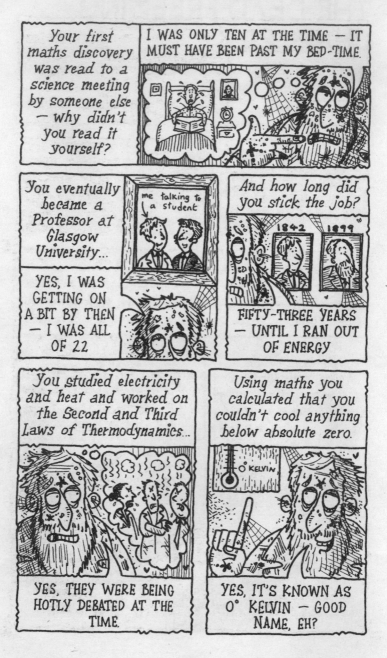

Your first maths discovery was read to a science meeting by someone else — why didn't you read it yourself?

I WAS ONLY TEN AT THE TIME — IT MUST HAVE BEEN PAST MY BED-TIME.

You eventually became a Professor at Glasgow University...

me talking to a student

YES, I WAS GETTING ON A BIT BY THEN — I WAS ALL OF 22

And how long did you stick the job?

1842   1899

FIFTY-THREE YEARS — UNTIL I RAN OUT OF ENERGY

You studied electricity and heat and worked on the Second and Third Laws of Thermodynamics...

YES, THEY WERE BEING HOTLY DEBATED AT THE TIME.

Using maths you calculated that you couldn't cool anything below absolute zero.

0° KELVIN

YES, IT'S KNOWN AS 0° KELVIN — GOOD NAME, EH?

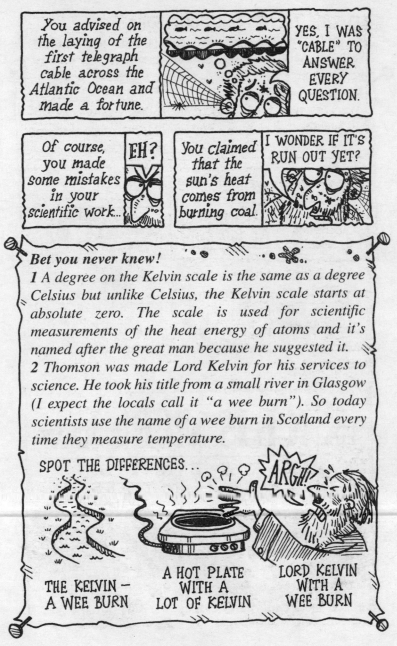

You advised on the laying of the first telegraph cable across the Atlantic Ocean and made a fortune.

YES, I WAS "CABLE" TO ANSWER EVERY QUESTION.

Of course, you made some mistakes in your scientific work...

EH?

You claimed that the sun's heat comes from burning coal.

I WONDER IF IT'S RUN OUT YET?

Bet you never knew!

1 A degree on the Kelvin scale is the same as a degree Celsius but unlike Celsius, the Kelvin scale starts at absolute zero. The scale is used for scientific measurements of the heat energy of atoms and it's named after the great man because he suggested it.

2 Thomson was made Lord Kelvin for his services to science. He took his title from a small river in Glasgow (I expect the locals call it "a wee burn"). So today scientists use the name of a wee burn in Scotland every time they measure temperature.

SPOT THE DIFFERENCES...

THE KELVIN – A WEE BURN

A HOT PLATE WITH A LOT OF KELVIN

ARGH!!

LORD KELVIN WITH A WEE BURN

WELCOME TO THE CHILL-OUT ZONE

So would you like to experience absolute zero (almost)? Well, what you need is a holiday in space...

Bet you never knew!
Away from the sun's heat, space is only a degree or two above absolute zero. It's so cold that pee ejected from a space loo freezes instantly into a pretty stream of golden crystals. When asked what was the most beautiful sight he had seen, one returning astronaut replied:

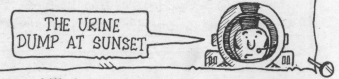

THE URINE DUMP AT SUNSET

For some chilled-out scientists this sort of thing is brrrrrilliant. They cool atoms for super-cool experiments by trapping them with magnetic forces. Did you know that electricity runs through the chilled-out atoms with scarcely any friction? Well that's just the start of the weird stuff...

THE **ICE IS NICE** COMPANY

P R E S E N T S...

Fancy a cool thrill?
Buy this super-cooled helium (it's the same gas they put in high-flying balloons) but it's cooled to −272.2° C (−485° F).
Amaze your friends and terrify the cat as it turns into a liquid and starts climbing the sides of the jar.

COOL!

THE SMALL PRINT
Don't drop your cat in the helium
or you might end up with a frozen pet!

Fancy an ice-cream?

Can't wait hours for it to freeze?
Try using this super-cold liquid nitrogen at −196° C (−393° F)! In 1997 a British scientist used this substance to make ice-cream in ten seconds! Children who sampled the ice-cream said it was "very nice" and a chef said:

IT'S NOT VERY RICH OR CREAMY, BUT IT DEFINITELY TASTES LIKE AN ICE-CREAM.

THE SMALL PRINT
The nitrogen won't spoil the taste. When it meets air it turns into nitrogen gas and floats away – and that's fine, because air is mostly nitrogen gas.

By the way, if you're thinking of making the ice-cream you should know that if you stick your finger in liquid nitrogen it'll freeze solid and break off. I guess that's what they call "a cold snap" – or do I mean ice-scream?

But talking about dipping bodies in liquid nitrogen, did you know that some people are planning to preserve their dead bodies in just this fashion?

Fearless reporter Harvey Tucker is just about to find out more. . .

43

HARVEY TUCKER'S BIG ADVENTURE

Fearless - me? Aw come off it! Okay - I'll come clean...

I've been writing for *Living on the Edge Magazine* for yonks. I've described how I bungee jumped from helicopters, dived with great white sharks and jogged across deserts. Lies, dam lies! The closest I've come to a shark is watching the Discovery channel on TV.

Well, they're *dangerous* aren't they?

ANGRY EDITOR

But when the magazine's editor found out about this she wasn't too sympathetic. She gave a nasty little smile and sent me off to write an in-depth undercover feature on cryogenics - that's when bodies get deep frozen.

Frankly I wasn't too tickled - I do feel the cold. But we Tuckers always bounce back and I soon hit on a real beaut plan! I decided to disguise myself as a dead body! My mate Sally Smart offered to pose as the bereaved rellie and do the natter — she's a real sport! All I had to do was lie back and listen. So I snacked up on five jumbo packets of crisps and vegemite sandwiches so I wouldn't feel too peckish in my coffin.

SALLY

44

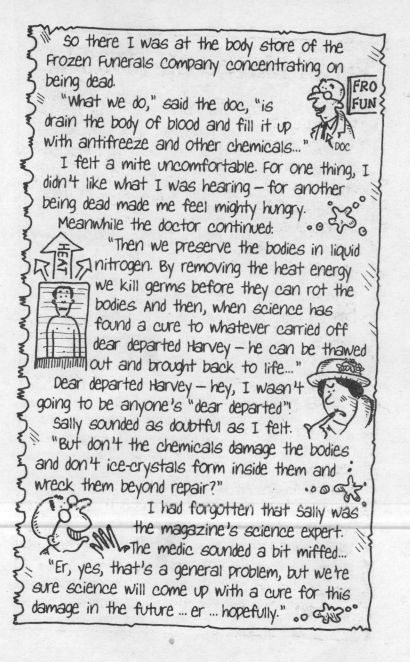

So there I was at the body store of the Frozen Funerals company concentrating on being dead.

"What we do," said the doc, "is drain the body of blood and fill it up with antifreeze and other chemicals..."

I felt a mite uncomfortable. For one thing, I didn't like what I was hearing – for another being dead made me feel mighty hungry.

Meanwhile the doctor continued:

"Then we preserve the bodies in liquid nitrogen. By removing the heat energy we kill germs before they can rot the bodies. And then, when science has found a cure to whatever carried off dear departed Harvey – he can be thawed out and brought back to life..."

Dear departed Harvey – hey, I wasn't going to be anyone's "dear departed"!

Sally sounded as doubtful as I felt.

"But don't the chemicals damage the bodies and don't ice-crystals form inside them and wreck them beyond repair?"

I had forgotten that Sally was the magazine's science expert. The medic sounded a bit miffed...

"Er, yes, that's a general problem, but we're sure science will come up with a cure for this damage in the future ... er ... hopefully."

45

Whilst they were yacking, I risked opening an eye and taking a butchers at the body store. I could see bodies in flasks – a chill ran through my veins.

I felt as cold as the bods.

"How much does it cost?" Sally was asking.

"That depends," replied the doc. "It's $100,000 for the full body but only $50,000 for the head – it's a cut-price offer."

Cut off – what?! Well, I freaked didn't I?

"Forget it, mate!" I yelled sitting up in my coffin.

ARGH!

The doctor screamed and ran off and Sally gave me a frosty look. She's been really cold to me ever since.

Cryogenics is popular in the USA and many bodies and heads have already been frozen. Some people have had their pet dogs preserved – I guess they're frozen Fidos. But some companies operating the service have gone bust and had their assets frozen (maybe it's the chilly economic climate) and the bodies thawed out with smelly results. I'm sure it's a thaw point all round.

Of course, you don't need to find a vat of liquid nitrogen to find a frozen body – there are plenty of well-preserved bodies in the polar regions at the ends of the Earth. Why not turn to the next ice-cool chapter and find out how they got there and what happens to the body when it gets low on vital heat energy. Yes, read on, you're about to make a chilling discovery...

KILLER COLD

This chapter is warmer than the last one, but it's still freezing cold. Later chapters will be hot enough to fry your fingertips but for now you're more likely to freeze them off! This chapter is full of cool killer facts about how lack of heat energy freezes water ... and people.

COULD YOU BE A SURGEON?

You're a surgeon. Your patient has a swelling blood vessel in his brain. Soon the blood vessel will burst and cause a killer build up of blood pressure. Your patient could die – *what can you do*? Better hurry up and decide…

a) Cut open the patient's skull and squirt the brain with liquid nitrogen to freeze it up and stop the blood moving.

b) Cut open the skull and pack ice cubes around the brain to reduce the swelling.

c) Pack the patient's body with ice until their body temperature is low, remove half their blood and then operate on the brain.

Answer:

c) Cooling the body slows it down so it needs less oxygen from the blood. (In fact, cooling can be used to treat severely injured people by giving their bodies a chance to heal naturally.) By draining the blood you reduce swelling and gain time to operate on the blood vessel. In the 1960s a Japanese brain surgeon chilled the brains of patients to 6°C (43°F), drained their blood and operated before warming the brains up with nice hot blood. I expect he needed a cool head.

47

Bet you never knew!

In 1983 a temperature of -89.2°C (-128.6°F) was recorded at the Russian Vostock Base, Antarctica. This was so cold that if you threw a mug of boiling tea in the air it would turn into a tea-flavoured ice lolly before it hit the ground!

Fancy going there for a holiday? Well, if so you'll enjoy chilling out in a hotel built out of solid ice! There really is such a place … here's how they might advertise it.

HAVE AN 'ICE DAY! AT THE
ICE HOTEL
NORTHERN SWEDEN

❄ A real cool place to stay!

❄ You're sure of a frosty reception! → HI!!

SORRY, WE DON'T DO HOT COCOA!

❄ Break the ice at the ice bar (yes the bar's made from ice too!) and the drinks are always on ice (they're served in containers made of ice).

❄ Relax in your luxury bedroom!

* * * * THE SMALL PRINT * * * *

1. Your bedroom and your bed are solid ice! Central heating might melt the hotel so your bedroom has to be freezing. You do get a comfy mattress and sleeping bag and we promise not to laugh if you wear a bobble hat in bed!   SHIVER!   SHAKE!

ICE HOTEL

2. Don't bother coming back - by the spring the hotel will have melted but we'll build a new one next winter we promise!

So what's this got to do with energy?

Killer energy fact file

NAME: Ice

HEAT!

LOCK!

"WOBBLE!"

THE BASIC FACTS:

1. As water cools it loses heat energy to the air.

2. At 0°C (32°F) the groups of atoms (molecules as scientists call them) that make up water lock together.

3. Ice still has heat energy and the frozen water molecules are still gently wobbling.

KILLER DETAILS: 1. If you added up all the heat energy in an ice cube there'd be enough to produce a flame hotter than a burning match.

2. When you make a snowball you crush the ice-crystals together and this movement energy turns to heat energy that melts some of the ice. The squishy water makes the ball easy to mould.

BEWARE – if the snowball hits your teacher he might go in for the kill!

GRRR!

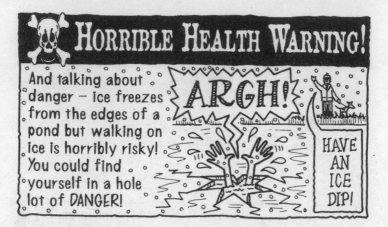

HORRIBLE HEALTH WARNING!

And talking about danger – ice freezes from the edges of a pond but walking on ice is horribly risky! You could find yourself in a hole lot of DANGER!

ARGH!

HAVE AN ICE DIP!

TEACHER'S TEA-BREAK TEASER

It's break-time. With luck your teacher will just be getting some milk from the fridge to put in her tea when you knock on the staffroom door…

IF THE SECOND LAW OF THERMODYNAMICS SAYS HEAT ALWAYS GOES FROM A WARM PLACE TO A COLD PLACE, HOW IS IT POSSIBLE FOR FRIDGES TO MOVE HEAT OUT FROM THE COLD FRIDGE TO THE WARM ROOM?

WHAT?

Answer:
Even if your teacher understands what you're talking about, explaining the answer will take her all break by which time the Second Law will have made sure that her tea is colder than a shivering Siberian snowman. But you could be in hot water!

HOW A FRIDGE WORKS

Fridge tubes contain a chemical that turns into a gas in the part of the tube that's inside the fridge. For this to happen the chemical needs heat energy so it sucks heat from the inside of the fridge.

⋅ THE "STAFFROOM" FRIDGE ⋅

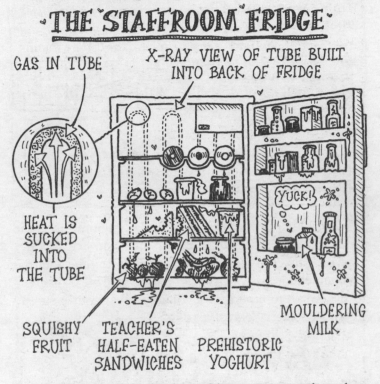

GAS IN TUBE

X-RAY VIEW OF TUBE BUILT INTO BACK OF FRIDGE

YUCK!

HEAT IS SUCKED INTO THE TUBE

SQUISHY FRUIT

TEACHER'S HALF-EATEN SANDWICHES

PREHISTORIC YOGHURT

MOULDERING MILK

In fact, fridges actually heat things up more than they cool things down! The gas is squashed into the tubes at the back of the fridge by a pump and this makes it form a liquid and release the heat energy it took from inside the fridge. And if you count the heat given out by the pump motor, fridges actually produce MORE heat than they ever suck out of your ice-cream.

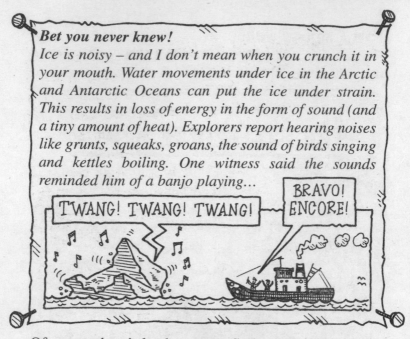

Bet you never knew!

Ice is noisy – and I don't mean when you crunch it in your mouth. Water movements under ice in the Arctic and Antarctic Oceans can put the ice under strain. This results in loss of energy in the form of sound (and a tiny amount of heat). Explorers report hearing noises like grunts, squeaks, groans, the sound of birds singing and kettles boiling. One witness said the sounds reminded him of a banjo playing...

TWANG! TWANG! TWANG!

BRAVO! ENCORE!

Of course there's loads more to find out about life in the cold, and who better to discover this than ace reporter Harvey Tucker? After his embarrassing failure with the cryogenics company Harvey's been packed off in disgrace to the Arctic to report on a polar survival course run by famous explorer Fergus Fearless...

HARVEY TUCKER'S BIG ADVENTURE

I told her I can't stand the cold!
Adventure - my bum!
I was stranded hundreds of miles from a decent bar. I was cold, I was hungry...

SHIVER!

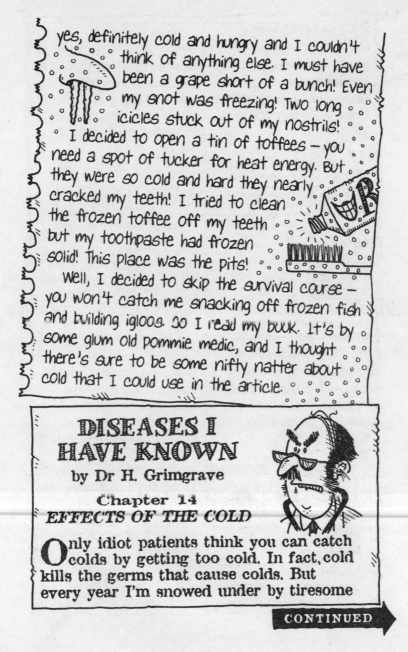

yes, definitely cold and hungry and I couldn't think of anything else. I must have been a grape short of a bunch! Even my snot was freezing! Two long icicles stuck out of my nostrils!

I decided to open a tin of toffees — you need a spot of tucker for heat energy. But they were so cold and hard they nearly cracked my teeth! I tried to clean the frozen toffee off my teeth but my toothpaste had frozen solid! This place was the pits!

Well, I decided to skip the survival course — you won't catch me snacking off frozen fish and building igloos. So I read my book. It's by some glum old pommie medic, and I thought there's sure to be some nifty natter about cold that I could use in the article.

DISEASES I HAVE KNOWN
by Dr H. Grimgrave

Chapter 14
EFFECTS OF THE COLD

Only idiot patients think you can catch colds by getting too cold. In fact, cold kills the germs that cause colds. But every year I'm snowed under by tiresome

CONTINUED

timewasters who claim they caught colds by being snowed under. I'm only a doctor but they still expect me to cure them!

Frostbite is a more likely outcome for people who get lost in snow. Blood vessels in the skin close to keep heat energy in the body. The nerve endings that feel things stop working, which is why extreme cold causes numbness: it's known as frostnip. Oxygen doesn't reach these areas and, of course, they begin to die. In severe cases this can cause blisters and blackening.

AFTER A WHILE THE AFFECTED AREA STARTS TO ROT AND SMELL.

Recently, my colleague Dr Sneak went on a skiing holiday. The silly idiot forgot his thermal socks – and developed frostbite in his big toe. It was just "toe" bad, ha ha.

I advised him on the telephone to avoid rubbing the toe – this may damage it.

DR SNEAK

"The thing to do," I said, "is to bathe the toe in warm water and see a doctor."

"But I am a doctor!" he protested.

So I told him to see a *proper* doctor.

In severe frostbite the affected bits actually drop off (these patients need to pull themselves together, ha, ha). Or the frost-bitten bit may be amputated (or "chopped off" as vulgar persons say). Any readers who have lost fingers and toes would be welcome to donate them to my private medical collection. I might pay a small fee just so long as it doesn't cost an arm and a leg.

More lethal than frostbite is cooling of the body (hypothermia [hi-po-ther-me-a] as we doctors term it). Of course, every winter I get an avalanche of malingerers who think feeling a bit chilly is going to kill them – no such luck I'm afraid! I'm always cool to them. Drink hot drinks and wrap up warm – that's my advice. Physical exercise helps – I always order a five mile run for children who complain of the cold. They generally stop snivelling after the first four miles!

Real hypothermia is likely to affect idiots who go out in the cold without warm clothing and they deserve everything they get. As their bodies cool they shiver violently. They think they're hot and feel like removing clothing.

TYPICAL IDIOT

As the brain cools it sees things. One idiot even rang me and said he thought he was a pack of cards! I told him I'd deal with him later. People suffering from hypothermia need to be warmed up slowly to avoid further damage to the body. But of course what they really deserve is a good roasting!

55

Well, cop that! Reading about hypo-what's-it gave me the shivers - AH NO! shivering's a sign of hypo-thingie! I snuggled in my sleeping bag and felt hot - isn't that hypo too? I decided to build my strength by eating a mega-de-luxe family-sized pizza but it had frozen rock-solid! The cold crept up on me until it seemed to chill the marrow of my bones. I wrote my farewell letters - goodbye cruel world! But then...

"Hold on!" I thought, "Fergus Fearless might have a web-site to tell me how to stay alive - it's worth a bo-peep."

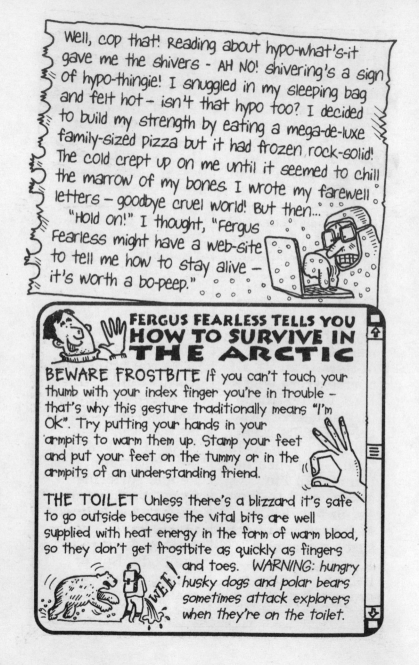

FERGUS FEARLESS TELLS YOU HOW TO SURVIVE IN THE ARCTIC

BEWARE FROSTBITE If you can't touch your thumb with your index finger you're in trouble - that's why this gesture traditionally means "I'm Ok". Try putting your hands in your armpits to warm them up. Stamp your feet and put your feet on the tummy or in the armpits of an understanding friend.

THE TOILET Unless there's a blizzard it's safe to go outside because the vital bits are well supplied with heat energy in the form of warm blood, so they don't get frostbite as quickly as fingers and toes. *WARNING:* hungry husky dogs and polar bears sometimes attack explorers when they're on the toilet.

WEE!

H-E-L-P! As soon as I read these words I needed the dunny! But, oh no, it was too dangerous! This place had got on my quince! So I got on my radio blower for help. And whilst I was waiting to be rescued, I crunched my way through the rest of the frozen toffees. It seemed a shame to waste 'em!

Bet you never knew!
1 Frostbite was a killer condition for early explorers who were trying to reach the North and South Poles. One day American Robert Peary (1856–1920) took off his boots and eight of his toes fell off. He later remarked:

A FEW TOES WERE NOT MUCH TO GIVE TO ACHIEVE THE POLE

Do you agree?
2 In 2000 a museum received an unusual donation. Major Michael Lane sent them five of his own fingers and eight of his toes. They had been lost to frostbite when he was climbing Mount Everest in 1976. "I don't think it was quite what they were expecting," remarked the gallant mountaineer.
3 In 1991 frostbite claimed both the hands of heroic Korean climber Kim Hong Bin on Mount McKinley, USA – but he made it to the top using his legs and teeth.

So you've read this chapter and you're an expert in dealing with deadly lack of heat energy (or "cold" as non-scientists say)? But before you move on to the next chapter, why not try your hand at this killer quiz? Could you survive the ultimate challenge and reach the North or South Pole?

COULD YOU BE A POLAR EXPLORER?

1 It's so cold that your breath has frozen and covered the inside of your hut with ice. What do you do?

a) Put up with it.

b) Melt the ice with a blow-torch.

c) Open a window.

2 Which food would give you the most energy?

a) Chocolate.

b) Spinach.

c) Greasy lumps of fat from a dead animal mixed with toffee and banana breakfast cereal.

3 You're starving hungry but you have no food left. You need food to keep warm – what do you eat first?

a) Your traditional Eskimo-style socks.

b) Your dogs.

c) Your little brother/sister.

4 When travelling to the South Pole what's the best place to store fuel for heat and cooking?

a) In blocks of ice.

b) In jars sealed with corks.

c) In jars with leather seals.

Answers:

1 a) It's all you can do. **b)** would use up vital fuel and may set fire to your hut and **c)** would make it colder.

2 c) When explorers Dave Mitchell and Stephen Martin walked to the North Pole in 1994 they actually ate this. The fat, or suet as it's called, gives you more energy for its weight than most other foods. Fancy a munch?

3 b) Choose a dog that seems weaker than the others. When you've eaten all your dogs you could eat **a)** because they're made of animal hair. WARNING: eating your brothers and sisters is cruel and may result in a long prison sentence.

4 b) Using ice to store fuel is really fuel-ish ... er ... foolish because you'll need fuel to make a fire to melt the ice to get at the fuel. In 1911 a British expedition led by Robert Falcon Scott (1868–1912) used **c)**, and a rival team led by Norwegian Roald Amundsen (1872–1928) used **b)**. Amundsen got to the South Pole first. Scott's leather seals froze and dropped off and the Brits ran out of fuel and died of cold. Their frozen bodies still lie in Antarctica where they perished.

The unlucky explorers were killed by the killer science of fuel and lack of heat energy. As any scientist will tell you, fuel is a form of stored energy and, by some power-fuel coincidence, the next chapter will have you firing on all cylinders... It really is a gas!

HORRIBLY POWERFUL FUEL

Without fuel – or the energy stored in fuel – the world would grind to a chilly halt. Fuels like gas, oil, coal and petrol store the vital energy that keeps you warm and cooks your supper…

…and fuel may well get you to school on time…

TROUBLE IN STORE

But fuels are just one way in which energy can be stored. Here are some other ways to store energy which are just about to cause disaster for the world's most accident-prone teacher.

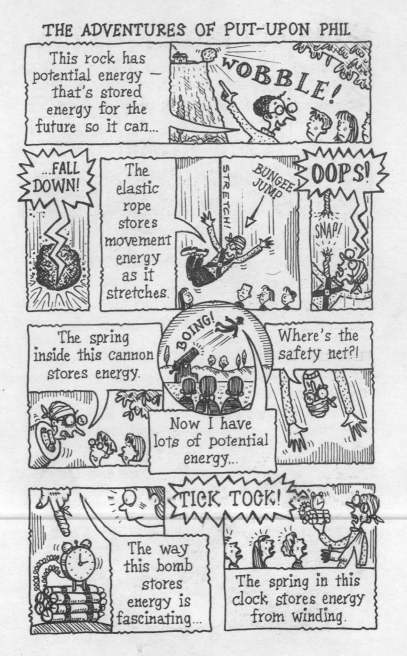

And the dynamite stores chemical energy... of course it's quite safe...

BOOM!

THAT'S IT – I QUIT!

THE FUEL FACTS

For thousands of years the only fuel for most people was wood to burn in fires. Open fires provided light and heat to roast a juicy hunk of dead mammoth. But around 3000 BC an Egyptian invented the candle. No one knows this person's name but it was a *flaming* good idea – here's how it worked.

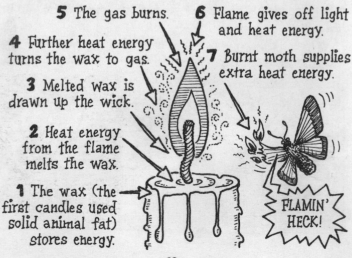

5 The gas burns.

6 Flame gives off light and heat energy.

4 Further heat energy turns the wax to gas.

7 Burnt moth supplies extra heat energy.

3 Melted wax is drawn up the wick.

2 Heat energy from the flame melts the wax.

1 The wax (the first candles used solid animal fat) stores energy.

FLAMIN' HECK!

62

Now the great thing about candles is that you can move them around, so they were really useful to take with you to bed if you were scared of the dark in the days before electricity. But you still need to make a flame to light the candle. Traditionally, people struck pieces of metal and flint to make sparks, but what was needed was a striking new idea...

In the 1850s Swedish inventor John Lundstrom invented the matches still used today. The energy is stored in the side of the box in the form of phosphorus (fos-for-rus). This substance burns when heated by the energy of the match striking the side. (If the match doesn't light it's probably on strike, ha ha.)

Anyway, phosphorus was discovered in 1669 in a revolting fashion. This story may shed some light on the subject.

A GLOW IN THE DARK

Hamburg, Germany 1677

"Yes, Herr Obermeyer, I'll tell you everything. Since you're the Mayor perhaps you can right this wrong."

And with these words, the old woman settled herself on a stool by the Mayor's fireplace and began her story.

"Sir, I'll be honest. My master, Hening Brandt, is not a good man. He is rude to us servants and grovels to people richer than himself. He married his first wife for her money, and by the time she'd died he'd spent it on science experiments. Aye, I'm not one to gossip but it's said he married the present Frau Brandt for her money too. He's always trying to make gold from cheap metals. What's that? He's an alchemist? Why yes, that's what he calls himself...

"One dark evening I was passing my master's laboratory. I was taking a clean suit to his room – oh dear, what a mess my master makes of his clothes with all those chemicals! And the smells from that room are better left imagined! He had buckets of – how can I put it politely? It was wee – rotting in some experiment."

The old woman screwed up her face in disgust.

"Of course we servants weren't allowed to clean in there, but the stink was horrible enough!

Then I heard his voice. Thinking he was calling me, I crept to the door. But my master was talking to himself...

"'It glows!' I heard him say 'It's the secret of how to make gold and I've found it in wee!'

"I peered into the room. It was dark but I could see his fat excited face in a strange light that came from a glowing flask. Then he saw me and in a second he had me by the throat. He slapped my face once, twice – for all his fat he's a big strong man. He told me that he'd do terrible things if I dared to tell anyone what I'd seen. I promised I wouldn't – I had to didn't I?

"And true to my word I've kept his secret for six years. I always think that a good servant sees everything and says nothing. And all that time my master tried to make gold from the substance. He tried and failed and tried and failed until he had spent all his wife's money.

"We began to be pestered by alchemists who wanted the secret of the glowing substance. How they heard of it I can't say – but my master had taken to boasting of his discovery in taverns. And to think – he had sworn *me* to silence!"

There was a crack, and shower of sparks leapt up the chimney from a log on the fire. The woman gave a little gasp and looked up in alarm as if expecting to see her master's angry face. Then she continued her story.

"One night my master was visited by a Herr Krafft. He offered to give my master money in return for the secret. But my master was sly as well as greedy. He wouldn't tell Herr Krafft how he made the glowing material but he promised to sell what he had. He added with a low laugh that he could make plenty more.

"I wanted to tell Herr Krafft that the substance was made of wee but I was afraid of my master's temper. So I sat quietly with my sewing. Suddenly there was a pounding on the door.

"It was Herr Kunckel, he was an alchemist who had called to see the strange substance a few days before. Herr Kunckel also wanted to buy some of the chemical but my master told him rudely that he'd failed to make any more. I heard my master whisper, 'yes, it's made of wee, now go away!'

"Then, looking flustered, he came back and closed his deal with Herr Krafft.

"After Herr Krafft left, my master began to dance. Soon he was slapping his legs and laughing fit to burst.

"His friend the innkeeper came round and my master ordered me to fetch wine. After a bottle or two my master was drunk. His fat face shone red and shiny in the firelight and his voice was loud and slurred as he boasted of how he had tricked Herr Krafft and Herr Kunckel.

"The innkeeper leaned forward and prodded my master's belly.

"'So what's this substance made of – you old crook?'

"My master exploded with laughter until his chins wobbled.

"'Wee' he snorted, 'left to rot and heated until it's just a white powder at the bottom of a flask – then heated again! Two hundred thalers – just think of it – two hundred silver thalers for a pot of wee!'

"My master laughed until he rocked backwards and forwards. Then he wiped his wet lips and clumsily tapped his nose.

"'Remember, old friend, not a word of this.' he hissed.

"Well Sir, I am sure you've heard what happened next – it was the talk of Hamburg. Herr Kunckel made his own glowing substance. And they do say that Herr Krafft made a fortune showing it to kings and queens all over Europe. And now Kunckel and Krafft are telling everyone that *they* discovered the chemical! My master was in a foul mood for days – he's been unbearable! And that's why I am here to testify that my master, Hening Brandt, made the discovery first.

"A good servant never offers an opinion but I must add a word of my own. Sir, I wish this substance had never been found! It's like an evil genie making men cruel and selfish and greedy so that they trick one another and tell lies. What's that? How can I prove what I say is true?"

The woman looked troubled.

"I'm only a poor serving woman – I have only my word – and this…"

She opened her bag and slowly drew out a small flask. The flask contained a powder that shone with the ghostly glow of green fire.

Bet you never knew!

1 When phosphorous atoms combine with oxygen in the air, the atoms give out their stored energy in the form of light. Although phosphorus is poisonous it was made into pills to cure stomach and lung diseases. The pills were useless and the people who ate them felt sick and began to glow in the dark.

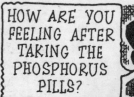

HOW ARE YOU FEELING AFTER TAKING THE PHOSPHORUS PILLS?

A LITTLE LIGHT-HEADED!

2 In 1890 a girl was smeared with phosphorus so that she could pretend to be a ghost during a seance (a gathering where ghosts are supposed to appear). The poison killed the girl, so perhaps she became a genuine ghost.

Today few Europeans and Americans use candles and open fires. (Mind you, it's rumoured that in power cuts mean-spirited teachers wrap themselves in woolly scarves and teach by the light of candles. Anything to avoid sending their pupils home.)

But mostly we rely on gas or electricity produced from coal, gas or oil. Now I expect you're keen to find out about these vital forms of energy, so we've invited an expert to answer your questions...

HORRIBLE SCIENCE QUESTION TIME
With Bernard Boyle of the Energy Department

All fossil fuels burn well. In power stations they're burnt to release heat energy to heat water and make steam...

Does it boil?

It's *Professor Boyle* to you! Oh you mean the water — yes!

The steam turns the blades of a turbine round. The turbine turns a powerful magnet and makes an electric current.

STEAM →

TURBINES — MAGNETS

The problem is that the fossil fuels and especially oil will be running out by the 2060's.

Did you say oil be running out?

No, I'll be here for another two hours!

GROAN!

Bet you never knew!
When it's pumped out of the ground by an oil rig, oil is a disgusting thick green-black slime called crude oil. Crude oil's full of chemicals such as paraffin and petrol and butane (used to fuel camping stoves). In the 1860s rock oil (a mixture including petrol) was sold as a medicine for toothache and corns. Yes, tank goodness you don't have to drink that!

Do you say...

I'M A RHINO-ANALYST...

AND I'M AN EXPERT STENCHER

WOW! I LIKE RHINOS TOO BUT YOUR FRIEND SOUNDS A REAL STINKER!

Answer:
DON'T YOU DARE!!! The killer scientists might attack you! A rhino-analyst studies smells in cooking gas. The actual gas doesn't smell, so smelly sulphur chemicals are added to the gas to make it pong so that people notice if they leave their gas taps on – this is called "stenching".

Although gas is often removed from rocks where there's oil, a cooking and lighting gas can also be made from coal. And I bet you never knew that this fact was discovered by a ingenious inventor with a terrible taste in hats...

Hall of Fame: William Murdock (1754–1839)
Nationality: Scottish

Mrs Murdock was furious...

"Ye greet daftie – luik wat ye've done to ma best china tea pot! It's ruined – ye greet muckle lump! It's nay guid noo! Ye've nay sense – tho ye be ma ane laddie!

(Mrs Murdock probably used other words that were too rude to repeat in a respectable book like this.)

Young William bowed his head and was just mumbling something about science experiments when the tea pot whizzed past his ear and smashed to pieces on the black iron stove behind him.

But he had actually made a vital discovery. By heating coal (yes, in his mum's tea pot) he had found out that you can make a gas that burns to produce heat and light energy. But then William always was a practical lad. Already he had built his own tricycle out of wood to get to school on time. This was surprising because:

1 He was keen to get to school.
2 The bicycle hadn't been invented yet!

When William was 23, he heard about a factory in England where they made the most powerful steam engines in the whole world. He was so excited that he *walked* hundreds of kilometres to the Soho Works in Birmingham to ask for a job. The boss, Matthew Boulton, was about to show William the door when the young man's hat fell off. It hit the floor with a solid clunk, as well it might since it was made of wood. Yes, the hat was one of William's inventions and it proved the lad was no wooden head.

For the rest of his life William worked for Matthew Boulton and his partner, Scottish steam engine inventor James Watt (1736–1819). He repaired steam engines all over the country but still found time to invent a steam-powered carriage and a method of using fish skin to remove cloudiness from beer (if your dad's into home brew this could spell doom for your pet goldfish).

William developed his coal gas idea. He began by heating coal in a tank and pumping it round pipes where the gas could be lit from special gas taps. First William lit the cottage in Cornwall where he was working and then the Soho works. Boulton was delighted by the discovery but he stopped William patenting his idea. Eventually other people copied him and he made no money from it.

THE FUEL CRISIS STARTS TO BITE

Remember what Bernard Boyle was saying about fossil fuels running out? You may have heard people talking about it. There's enough coal underground to keep us warm and cosy until about 2160 but by the 2000's oil and gas were running out in a hurry and the world was guzzling them like they were going out of fashion. For some scientists the answer was to think small – I mean very, very small...

Killer energy fact file

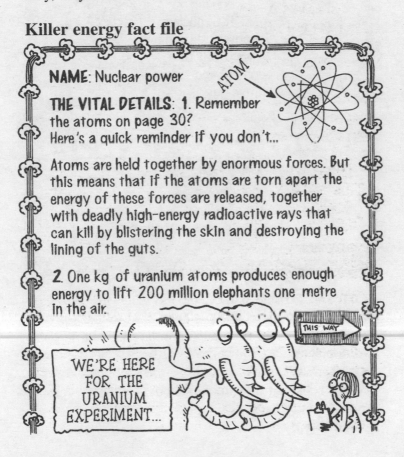

NAME: Nuclear power

THE VITAL DETAILS: 1. Remember the atoms on page 30? Here's a quick reminder if you don't...

ATOM

Atoms are held together by enormous forces. But this means that if the atoms are torn apart the energy of these forces are released, together with deadly high-energy radioactive rays that can kill by blistering the skin and destroying the lining of the guts.

2. One kg of uranium atoms produces enough energy to lift 200 million elephants one metre in the air.

THIS WAY

WE'RE HERE FOR THE URANIUM EXPERIMENT...

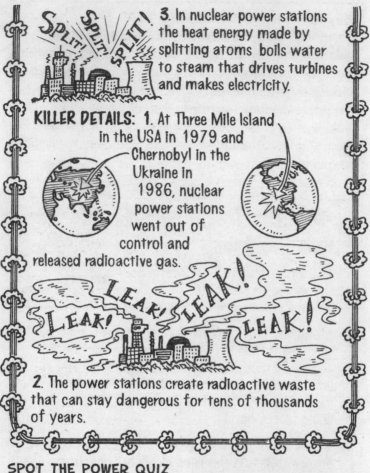

3. In nuclear power stations the heat energy made by splitting atoms boils water to steam that drives turbines and makes electricity.

KILLER DETAILS: 1. At Three Mile Island in the USA in 1979 and Chernobyl in the Ukraine in 1986, nuclear power stations went out of control and released radioactive gas.

2. The power stations create radioactive waste that can stay dangerous for tens of thousands of years.

SPOT THE POWER QUIZ

Some unusual materials have been used to make power. Have you the brain-power to spot the fuel that no one's ever tried?

1 Dead cows
2 Waste cooking oil from chip shops
3 Smelly rotten eggs
4 Used nappies

Answer:

3 But who "nose" what might happen in the future? As for the others, in 2000…

1 Some English power stations were making electricity from burning the remains of diseased cows. I suppose that's what they call moo-clear energy.

2 A man in Manchester, England ran his car on oil from his local chip shop that had been changed chemically into diesel oil. I suppose he could have run it on oranges but then he'd have run out of juice, ha ha.

4 French cement companies were burning the nappies to fire their cement-making kilns.

You can also make power from wind, waves, tides and solar power (that's the heat and light of the sun). These natural types of energy are called "renewable" because there's always more of them being made. And deep within the Earth there's another type of renewable energy: here's how YOU can tap into it…

HOW TO BUILD YOUR OWN
GEOTHERMAL POWER STATION

INTRODUCTION

Geothermal power uses the mass of molten rock thousands of metres under your feet to make heat energy. This power actually makes it possible to grow bananas in Iceland (in heated greenhouses)

MOLTEN ROCK

HEAT!

PLANET EARTH

so why not have a bash at building your own geothermal power station!

- No more nasty energy bills!
- Piping hot water for ever!
- No cost except for the few 100 million that you spent building your power station.

Some of these instructions may not be totally sensible. You're advised to read them carefully first!

WHAT YOU WILL NEED...

TWO DRILL RIGS

HEAVY LIFTING GEAR, BULLDOZERS, BUILDING MATERIALS, ETC.

SEVERAL KILOMETRES OF PIPES

VERY RICH, UNDERSTANDING PARENTS

AN OLYMPIC SIZED SWIMMING POOL OR PRIVATE LAKE.

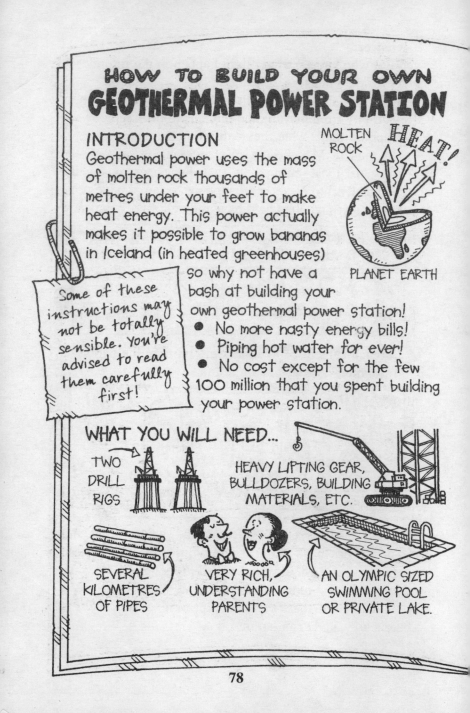

HOT ROCKS

INSTRUCTIONS

1. Set up your drill rigs and drill 7 km down until you reach some rocks that are hot enough to boil water.

2. Don't forget to push down the pipes into the holes after your drills.

HOUSE

PIPES

3. Remember to link up the pipes from your second bore hole with the hot water system of your house. I expect your friend's parents will be delighted to have their homes plumbed in too!

4. Now for the FUN bit! Link up the pipes to your first rig to the swimming pool and turn on the taps so the water rushes down into the first bore hole.

POOL

5. Superheated hot water will rush up the second bore hole and into your hot water system! Warning: you might need to adjust the pressure or your radiators may explode!

BOILING WATER

THE SMALL PRINT

If molten rock oozes from your bore holes you've created a volcano that could bury your neighbourhood and school under thousands of tonnes of red hot lava. This may be a good moment to leave the country.

WHOOPS!

Bet you never knew!
If your geothermal power station doesn't work there's a simple way to tackle the energy shortage: use less energy. Simply switch off those electrical gadgets left on stand-by – that'll save lots of power and I am sure that your dad won't mind losing the chance to video Trainspotter's Weekly. *Then you could turn down the heating and put on a warm jumper instead.*

And if you're cold you can rub your hands together. Remember how the drilled cannon made heat on page 31? Yes, that's right – in the same way, your hands rub together and the rubbing force (known as friction) turns movement energy into heat energy – easy-peasy!

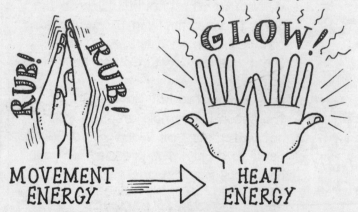

MOVEMENT ENERGY ⟹ HEAT ENERGY

Mind you, you'll find plenty of movement energy in the next chapter. In fact, it's just about to move off *now*!

NEXT CHAPTER

THE POWER TO MOVE YOU

Look out the window and you're sure to see something moving. You might see a cat chasing a mouse, or a dog chasing the cat, or children chasing the dog ... or the neighbours chasing the children or maybe everyone being chased by a killer Tyrannosaurus.

Well, they've all got something in common and it's called...

KILLER EXPRESSIONS

Do you say...

I STUDY KINETIC ENERGY

MY CAT'S GOT LOADS OF KITTY ENERGY!

Answer:
Don't show off the paw state of your knowledge. Kinetic (ki-net-tic) energy is the scientific name for movement energy. That's right – every move you make is powered by kinetic energy.

Bet you never knew!

Any kind of kinetic energy loses heat energy. If you don't believe me, try going for a run...

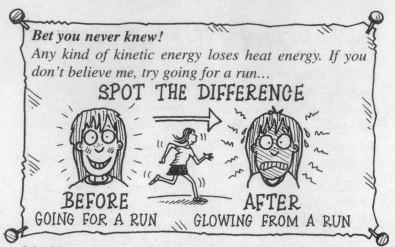

SPOT THE DIFFERENCE

BEFORE
GOING FOR A RUN

AFTER
GLOWING FROM A RUN

Machines also lose loads of heat, as you'll discover on page 92.

Kinetic energy moves caterpillars and cars and comets and ... well, everything, really. It even powers monster waves known as mega-tsunami (meg-a-tu-nar-me). Vast landslides into the sea provide kinetic energy for killer waves. They sweep across the ocean and arrive at the opposite shore half a kilometre high! But DON'T PANIC! Waves this big happen once in tens of thousands of years. Anyway, here's how to make your own model mega-tsunami ... without wrecking your house too badly.

Dare you discover ... how movement energy works?

You will need:

A TORCH

A WASHING UP BOWL OF WATER (IDEALLY THIS SHOULD BE PLACED IN THE KITCHEN SINK AND NOT OVER YOUR BROTHER/SISTER'S HEAD.)

What you do:
1 Wait until it's dark. Switch on the torch and hold it about 60 cm above the bowl.

2 Set the mixer tap so that a drop of water falls into the basin. (Or you could pick up a drop on your finger and let it fall from about 30 cm into the bowl.)

What do you notice?
a) Ripples spread out from the middle and then disappear.
b) Ripples move inwards from the side.
c) The ripples spread out to the sides and then move back.

Answer:
c) Did you spot the faint returning ripples? The kinetic energy of the falling drop makes ripples of movement energy through the water. The ripple loses energy to the sides and this makes it appear fainter as it returns to the centre.

Bet you never knew!
Sound energy is waves (like water waves) of movement energy in the air caused by noise – like your favourite music.

83

MAGIC MACHINES

The idea behind many hand-operated machines is to make life a bit easier by saving us energy. For example, using a tin-opener uses less energy than the alternative…

But many machines need even less human energy. These are machines that are powered by fuel energy, and right now it's time to meet the grand-daddy of all these types of machine…

HI-TECH MAGAZINE AD 100

HAVE A BALL!

Enjoy a spin with this exciting steam powered toy designed by Hero of Alexandria.

Movement energy of escaping steam makes the ball spin round.

Steam forced into pipes from boiler

Fire makes heat energy

Water heated up in boiler

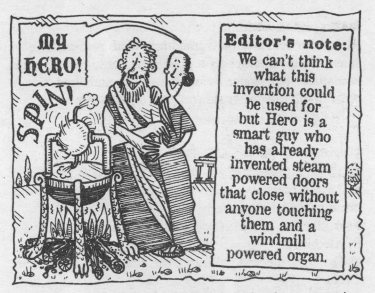

This idea might have set Roman technology steaming ahead. Just think – the Romans might have built steam trains and steam ships … but they didn't. As the magazine said, no one knew what to do with steam engines and the Romans weren't that bothered about saving muscle energy. Not whilst they had lots of slaves to do all the hard work.

It took another 1,600 years for an inventor named Thomas Savery (1650–1715) to reinvent the idea. One evening he drank a bottle of wine. He was too drunk to throw the bottle away – so he chucked it on the fire.

Steam puffed from the bottle and Savery was just sober enough to see that the remaining wine was turning to steam. So the boozy boffin pulled the bottle from the fire and stuck it in water to cool it down and then, to his amazement, the water was sucked into the bottle!

But what was going on?

COULD YOU BE A SCIENTIST?

So what do *you* think was causing this effect?

a) As the bottle cooled it grew slightly larger and this made room for the water.

b) As the air cooled it took up less space so the water flooded in.

c) The hot wine was pulling in the water by a mysterious force.

> **Answer:**
> **b)** When air has heat energy it pushes outwards, remember? As the air cools it takes up less space.

Savery worked this out and designed engines for pumping water from mines. Over the next 80 years inventors like Thomas Newcomen (1663–1729) and James Watt improved the steam engine until it could power any kind of machinery, and transport like trains and ships. The world was transformed, and all because a tipsy scientist had a lot of bottle.

Here's one of Watt's inventions – Watt an invention, eh? It's a wonderful way to turn heat energy into movement energy (that's the First Law of Thermodynamics from page 18).

86

WATT STEAM ENGINE

③ Piston passes movement energy to wheel

④ Drive belt transfers movement energy to machinery.

WHAT'S THIS MACHINE, WATT?

THIS IS WHAT I CALL MY WATT STEAM ENGINE

WHAT D'YOU MEAN WATT, WATT?

WHAT? WHAT WATT?

SPIN!

② Heat energy boils water to steam. Steam has movement energy.

① Energy stored in the form of coal. Coal burned to make heat energy.

A FEW FACTS TO GET STEAMED UP ABOUT...

1 Inventors were fascinated by steam engines. In the 1730s an 11-year-old boy named John Smeaton (1724–1794) was taken to see one of Newcomen's machines. He was so excited he built a model steam engine and used it to pump out his dad's goldfish pond. Don't try this at home!

You'll be pleased to know that John survived the punishment he got from his dad and grew up to be a famous engineer who built canals and lighthouses.

2 Inventors like William Murdock built steam carriages that ran on the road like cars today. In 1801 Murdock's pal, inventor Richard Trevithick (1771–1833), built his own steam carriage and took it for a spin. It broke down, but the inventor managed to fix it and went to the pub to celebrate. Unfortunately he left the fire on – the boiler boiled dry and the engine exploded. That must have been a BLASTED nuisance!

3 In 1894 inventor Hiram Maxim (1840–1916) built a giant plane with wings 38 metres across powered by steam engines. The engines weren't powerful enough to get the heavy plane flying. The plane managed to get a few centimetres into the air before crashing into a crumpled wreck. I expect Maxim got a bit steamed up about the accident.

But the most successful use for steam power turned out to be the steam turbine. As you discovered on page 71 – turbines are used to make electricity in power stations. But that proved to be the least of their uses – as you're about to find out:

Hall of Fame: Charles Parsons (1854–1931)
Nationality: Irish

Young Charles was born with a silver spoon in his mouth. NO, he didn't get a valuable bit of cutlery stuck in his gob! He was born filthy rich. His dad was a science-mad astronomer who happened to be the Earl of Rosse and owned his own castle. In 1845 the Earl built the world's largest telescope – at an astronomical cost. But the 15 metre monster proved a real big mistake since you could only use it when the sky was clear and in that part of Ireland it was usually raining.

Young Charles was too rich to go to school – so like James Joule he had his own personal teacher. Charles became interested in science and began to invent machines. He built a steam-powered carriage and gave his brothers rides. One day he took his aunt for a ride but she fell off the machine and died.

Charles joined a company that built steam engines. He enjoyed his work so much that when he got married his idea of a romantic honeymoon was dragging his bride off to watch the testing of his newly invented turbines on a miserably cold lake. Charles came away with a lot of scientific data and his wife came away with a nasty dose of fever.

In the 1880s Charles developed his idea for the turbine. The idea was very simple: hot steam energy powered small turning blades. In fact, the blades turned very fast and Charles realized that they could be used to turn a propeller and power a ship. Here's what happened next…

The secret diary of Rear-Admiral Lord Blewitt

1894 ~ I've just had a visit from that inventor chappie Parsons. Perfect crack-pot, just like his father! I've never heard such piffle and humbug! He says he can build a ship that sails at 34 knots - that's faster than any ship afloat! Parsons says he's got a working model but I told him in no uncertain terms that nothing is faster than an ordinary steam engine. Personally, though, I can't see what's wrong with wind-power - it was good enough when I was a boy! ∘∘

1895 ~ Yet another letter from that blasted nuisance Parsons. He's been pestering my fellow admirals with his half-cracked ideas. Can't he take NO for an answer? That fellow should be keel-hauled and flogged with the cat! His letter is full of scientific balderdash. He says he's built an actual boat now and he wants to show it off to us.
   That's out of the question!!! We admirals have more important things to do - like going for cruises!

1896 - Please excuse the shaky writing - I am in a state of shock. Today was Fleet Review Day. Every year we admirals watch proudly as our great fleet steams past and raise a glass of port to Her Majesty's good health! But not today. Oh no...

Blow me if the whole proceedings weren't completely ruined by a little boat dashing past at 34 knots! I was so taken aback I began to splutter and my false teeth fell out! Poor old Admiral Snuff was so upset he spent the whole day peering through the wrong end of his telescope!

I took a look through my own glass and saw that confounded blighter Parsons on the fast boat. He was actually grinning and waving! If I'd had my way our warships would have blown him out of the water! But, er ... no one could catch him, actually! I'm afraid he left even our fastest ships astern.

My fellow admirals are talking about ordering these new-fangled turbines. It seems that our entire navy has just become out of date! I have a real sinking feeling about all this...

91

You'll be pleased to know that Parsons became rich and famous although he later wasted most of his money trying to make diamonds out of graphite – that's the substance used to make pencil lead. Oh well, no doubt he thought he was on the write lines.

THE ULTIMATE FREEBIE

Mind you, for hundreds of years scientists having been trying to build an even more powerful machine. A machine that *never* needs any new energy! A machine that once it starts will never, ever stop! I suppose that's what our hungry reporter pal Harvey Tucker would call "the ultimate free lunch". Scientists call it "perpetual motion".

BUT HOLD ON, DIDN'T YOU SAY ON PAGE 18 THAT THE SECOND LAW SAYS THAT EVERYTHING LOSES ENERGY IN THE FORM OF HEAT AND THAT MEANS YOU HAVE TO KEEP PUTTING MORE ENERGY INTO IT?

A VERY ALERT READER

Hey, that's right! And what's more, as I said earlier, movement energy leads to a loss of heat energy and this means that sooner or later any machine will always run out of energy. In 1824 French scientist Nicolas Carnot (1796–1832) worked out that steam engines will never work perfectly for this reason. But I didn't say that perpetual motion worked, did I? Mind you, it took a while for scientists to figure this out...

THE SCIENTIST'S FRIEND
Problem Page with Professor Frank Helper

Are you a scientist with an embarrassing problem? Do you feel it would help to talk to someone who cares? If so write to me and no one need know your secret except, of course, our 567,000 readers! This week – perpetual motion...

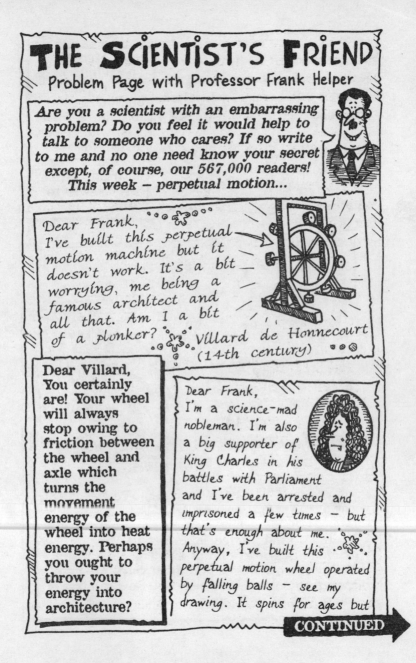

Dear Frank,
I've built this perpetual motion machine but it doesn't work. It's a bit worrying, me being a famous architect and all that. Am I a bit of a plonker?
Villard de Honnecourt (14th century)

Dear Villard,
You certainly are! Your wheel will always stop owing to friction between the wheel and axle which turns the movement energy of the wheel into heat energy. Perhaps you ought to throw your energy into architecture?

Dear Frank,
I'm a science-mad nobleman. I'm also a big supporter of King Charles in his battles with Parliament and I've been arrested and imprisoned a few times – but that's enough about me. Anyway, I've built this perpetual motion wheel operated by falling balls – see my drawing. It spins for ages but

CONTINUED →

then it stops. Why? Why? My head is spinning faster than my wheel – help me! Yours nobly, Edward Somerset The 2nd Marquis of Worcester (1601-1667)

Dear Marquis
The falling balls have no effect on your lordship's wheel. The wheel – er, I mean real – reason it stops is friction. See my answer to Villard.

Dear Frank,
I've gotta this bellissima perpetual motion machine! It's powered by de wind power and it's perfectissimo except for one tiny detail – it wonna work! I'd be humbly grateful for ever for your most kind advice.

Marco Zimara (Italy 1500s)

TURNING SAIL SQUEEZES DE BELLOWS TO MAKE MORE OF DE WIND.

WIND BLOWS THE SAILS ROUND

Dear Marco,
My most kind advice is, forget it! Your machine is a load of hot air! The sails lose energy from friction and don't have enough energy to squeeze the bellows. So I'm afraid you're out of puff, pal.

94

Yes, perpetual motion is about as likely as a puppy dog that doesn't pee in your slippers. Italian mega-genius Leonardo da Vinci (1452–1519) put it a bit more elegantly:

Oh you students of eternal motion! How many futile things have you created while searching for it.

And old Leo ought to know – he built his own machine which (please don't faint with surprise) didn't work.

Italian scientist Gerolamo Cardano (1501–1576) used maths to figure out that perpetual motion was impossible. Gerolamo led an exciting life. He was brought up by his strict grandmother who was cruel to him when he was naughty. (I hope your granny is a bit less vicious!) Gerolamo became a doctor and a scientist who claimed (rightly) that fire isn't a substance as people thought at the time, but then he found himself facing a fearsome fiery fate...

In 1570 he was arrested by the Church for using his interest in astrology (star signs) to speculate about religion. He was threatened with torture and burning to death unless he confessed he was wrong. Should he confess? It was a burning question. Clever Cardano did the sensible thing and he was released.

But later on his son murdered someone and had his head chopped off. Gerolamo fell out with his second son and asked the government to banish him to another city as "a youth of evil habits". Hopefully your dad is a bit less strict with you!

So there you are – perpetual motion is impossible. The laws of energy just won't allow it.

But what's this?

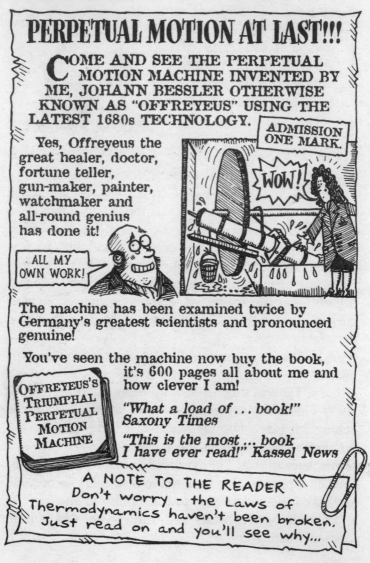

96

CONFESSION

I, Gretel Braun, the servant girl of Johann Bessler, confess that my master is a crook and his machine was built to trick foolish people out of their money. He spent his wife's savings building this machine but he wouldn't let anyone look at its insides — not even the scientists who said it was genuine. And why? Because there's a handle next door that turns the wheel! I should know — I had to crank that flipping handle every time people came to see the machine.

Ouch my poor back!

PS Please don't execute me — I was only doing my job!

Yes, Johann's machine relied on good old-fashioned muscle power. And that brings us to the next chapter. Actually I'm not going to tell you what's in it because I don't want to spoil the surprise.

But here's a hint... It's hot, it's sweaty and it's all yours...

HOT, SWEATY BODY BITS

This chapter is about how your body uses energy. Yes, this is the chapter in which the going gets tough. And you know what that means? The tough get going – and Harvey Tucker slobs out with a bucket of popcorn in front of the telly...

Killer energy fact file

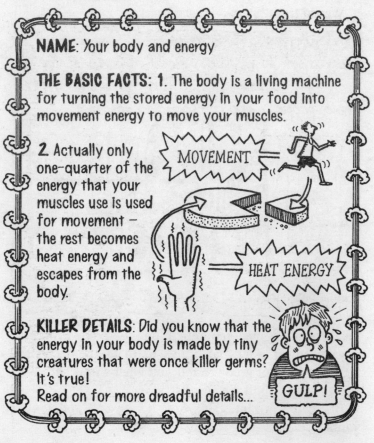

NAME: Your body and energy

THE BASIC FACTS: 1. The body is a living machine for turning the stored energy in your food into movement energy to move your muscles.

2. Actually only one-quarter of the energy that your muscles use is used for movement – the rest becomes heat energy and escapes from the body.

MOVEMENT

HEAT ENERGY

KILLER DETAILS: Did you know that the energy in your body is made by tiny creatures that were once killer germs? It's true!
Read on for more dreadful details...

GULP!

WORKING UP A SWEAT

Tough exercise is all in a day's work for athletes. In 2000, marathon runner Tegla Laroupe from Kenya said she took up running because she had to walk 10 km to school and was punished if she was late. Soon she was running 192 km a week. That's like running to school and all the way home again and all the way to school a second time. And doing it all again in the afternoon. And doing this every school day.

Wanna try it?

And speaking of exercise, here's a few killer holidays Harvey Tucker wouldn't be seen dead on (well, if he tried them he might be dead on them)…

4. If you die during the dance marathon you get disqualified.

IMPORTANT ANNOUNCEMENT

We've just found out that dance marathons have been BANNED in the USA since 1937 after several people went mad with tiredness. This holiday has been cancelled! Anyone who has booked will get a full refund ... that's if they can find where we've hidden the money.

Mind you, in the 1940s, dance marathons continued to be held in secret…

SICKENING SHIP SHINDIG SUNK!

NEW YORK NEWS

Cops raided an illegal dance marathon. The dancers might have been prancing to prison but the organisers herded them still dancing onto vans. After a can-can in the van it was a quick hop to the docks and a shuffle to a ship to take them outside US territory. But once at sea it was take your partners for the fling (your lunch) as seasickness had the dancers fox-trotting for the sides. Said one dancer, "It's heaving out there, 'scuse me gotta dash!"

HORRIBLE SCIENCE

FITNESS HOLIDAYS

DANCE **M**ARATHONS TOO *SOFT* FOR YOU? WHY NOT TRY THE

WESTERN STATES ENDURANCE RUN?!

YOU'VE GOT TO RUN 161 KM (100 MILES) IN LESS THAN 30 HOURS. YOU HAVE TO RUN UP MOUNTAINS AND AVOID RATTLESNAKES.

WARNING! YOUR BODY WILL DRY OUT IN THE HEAT AND YOU MAY LOSE 7% OF YOUR WEIGHT.

← START
FINISH →

AND WHILE YOU'RE AT IT, WHY NOT TRY THE

HAWAII IRONMAN COMPETITION?

SPLASH!
PEDAL!
STRIDE!

1 Swim	2 Cycle	3 Run a marathon
3.86 km	180 km	42.2 km
(2.4 miles)	(112 miles)	(26.2 miles)

WARNING! WE'VE ALLOWED A DAY FOR THE *WHOLE COMPETITION* SO YOU'D BEST HURRY OR YOU'LL MISS YOUR FLIGHT AND HAVE TO SWIM HOME ACROSS THE **P**ACIFIC **O**CEAN.

But all this energy raises a sensational scientific suggestion – how exactly do our bodies turn stored food energy into action-packed movement energy? How can a stodgy old school dinner help you turn in a world athletic running record? (And we're not talking about getting the squirts and having to dash for the loo.)

FIRST THE THEORIES...

1 Three hundred years ago scientists believed the muscles contained gunpowder that exploded to make them move. This idea wasn't as silly as it sounds because gunpowder is a form of stored energy and the muscles do use stored food energy (see below if you don't believe me). Of course, the idea was soon exploded.

2 French chemist Antoine Lavoisier (1743–1794) was interested in burning and breathing and pointed out that you breathe more when you work hard. Well, blow me if he wasn't right! Lavoisier reckoned that some kind of burning was going on in the lungs to change food into energy.

3 Then another scientist, Joseph Lagrange (1736–1813) said that if the lungs burnt food they'd catch fire. Hopefully your lungs won't do this – not even when you've eaten a really hot chilli.

4 German scientist Justus von Liebig (1803–1873) reckoned that the body's vital force moved the muscles.

But none of these clever and very thoughtful scientists grasped the truth. The answer to how the body uses energy is a small detail – how small? Oh, about 0.02 mm across. It's called a cell, and to find out more why not read this rare copy of HOW YOUR BODY WORKS by the famous Dr Jekyll and Mr Hyde. Apparently Dr Jekyll's quite nice but when he drinks a potion he turns into a blood-crazed killer monster...

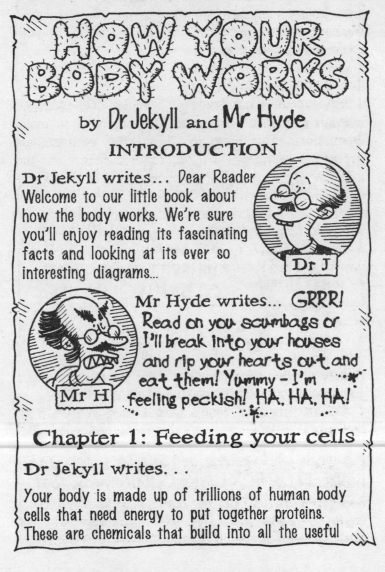

HOW YOUR BODY WORKS
by Dr Jekyll and Mr Hyde

INTRODUCTION

Dr Jekyll writes... Dear Reader Welcome to our little book about how the body works. We're sure you'll enjoy reading its fascinating facts and looking at its ever so interesting diagrams...

Dr J

Mr Hyde writes... GRRR! Read on you scumbags or I'll break into your houses and rip your hearts out and eat them! Yummy – I'm feeling peckish! HA, HA, HA!

Mr H

Chapter 1: Feeding your cells

Dr Jekyll writes. . .

Your body is made up of trillions of human body cells that need energy to put together proteins. These are chemicals that build into all the useful bits that make up the body. Every cell is a teeny-weenie living machine that makes power in hundreds of tiny units called **mitochondria** **(mi-toe-con-dree-a).** Mitochondria make energy using glucose — it's a very tasty type of sugar found in foods such as flour, bread,

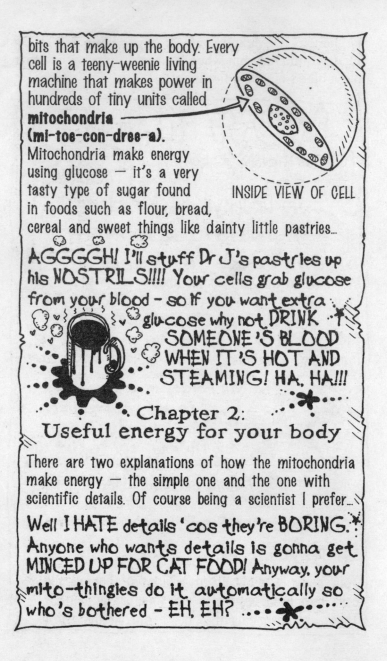

INSIDE VIEW OF CELL

cereal and sweet things like dainty little pastries...

AGGGGH! I'll stuff Dr J's pastries up his NOSTRILS!!!! Your cells grab glucose from your blood - so if you want extra glucose why not DRINK SOMEONE'S BLOOD WHEN IT'S HOT AND STEAMING! HA, HA!!!

Chapter 2:
Useful energy for your body

There are two explanations of how the mitochondria make energy — the simple one and the one with scientific details. Of course being a scientist I prefer...

Well I HATE details 'cos they're BORING. Anyone who wants details is gonna get MINCED UP FOR CAT FOOD! Anyway, your mito-thingies do it automatically so who's bothered - EH, EH? ....

I've drawn a nice clear diagram to make the process easy to understand.

HOW CELLS MAKE ENERGY

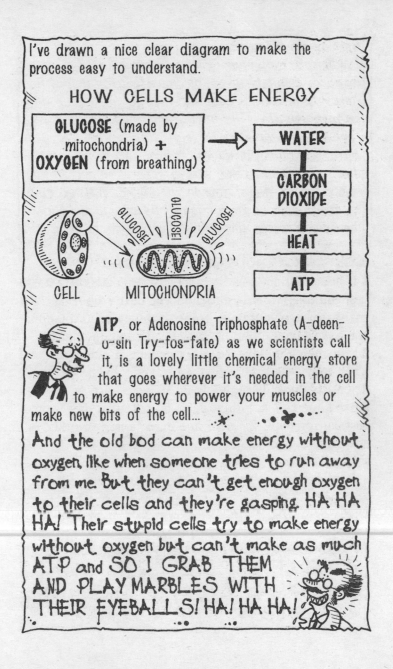

GLUCOSE (made by mitochondria) + OXYGEN (from breathing) →

WATER

CARBON DIOXIDE

HEAT

ATP

GLUCOSE! GLUCOSE! GLUCOSE!

CELL   MITOCHONDRIA

ATP, or Adenosine Triphosphate (A-deen-o-sin Try-fos-fate) as we scientists call it, is a lovely little chemical energy store that goes wherever it's needed in the cell to make energy to power your muscles or make new bits of the cell...

And the old bod can make energy without oxygen, like when someone tries to run away from me. But they can't get enough oxygen to their cells and they're gasping. HA HA HA! Their stupid cells try to make energy without oxygen but can't make as much ATP and SO I GRAB THEM AND PLAY MARBLES WITH THEIR EYEBALLS! HA! HA HA!

105

Bet you never knew!
1 When the cells make energy without using oxygen, lactic acid builds up in the muscles. You'll find the same chemical in sour milk – so getting cramp and burning muscles is like having your muscles filled with sour milk. No wonder you feel a little sour.
2 ATP contains phosphate, a form of phosphorous – that's the chemical that was discovered in pee. At this exact second there's about 90 ml of ATP sloshing around in your body and your cells have to make it all the time to keep you alive.

MIGHTY MYSTERIOUS MITOCHONDRIA

1 Inside you right now are about 10,000,000,000,000,000 (ten million billion) mitochondria busily churning out energy to keep your body going. But they're so small that you can fit one billion of them inside a grain of sand.

2 Mitochondria look like very tiny brown-red worms and when they make more of themselves they spilt in half. Scientists think that mitochondria were once germs that moved into cells a billion years ago. At first they were a pest but somehow the cells and mitochondria worked out how to live together...

OKAY, SO I PROVIDE FOOD AND SHELTER...

YEAH, AND I MAKE YOU ENERGY.

IT'S A DEAL!

And now every time you eat and every time you breathe you are doing it to feed alien life-forms hiding in your body!

3 You get your mitochondria from your mum. That's because the mitochondria in your cells are descended from a tiny egg made by your mum. Actually your energy level depends on lots of things like health and diet, but basically you get your energy from your mum!

MASSIVE MUSCLES

The part of your body that *really* needs energy is your muscles. It doesn't matter whether your muscles are bulging and beefy or you look like a stick insect on a diet. Your muscles are where your body turns stored chemical energy from ATP into movement energy.

And now for some facts you can muscle into…

Killer energy fact file

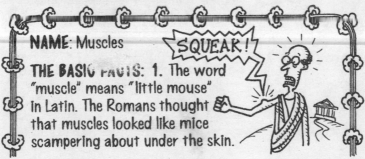

NAME: Muscles

SQUEAK!

THE BASIC FACTS: 1. The word "muscle" means "little mouse" in Latin. The Romans thought that muscles looked like mice scampering about under the skin.

2. All muscles are made of fibres that shorten in response to nerve signals from the brain. When the fibres relax so does the muscle.

SHORTENED!

3. Here are the main types of muscle.

RELAXED!

DIGEST! DIGEST!

MOVE! MOVE!

SMOOTH muscles make moves you can't control like shifting the food in your guts. These muscles aren't too strong.

STRIPED muscles move your body. You can control these.

HELP!!!

KILLER DETAILS: Muscles often come in pairs with opposing jobs — your biceps bends your arm and your triceps straightens it, for example. Some body builders develop such huge biceps that they can't straighten their arms properly.

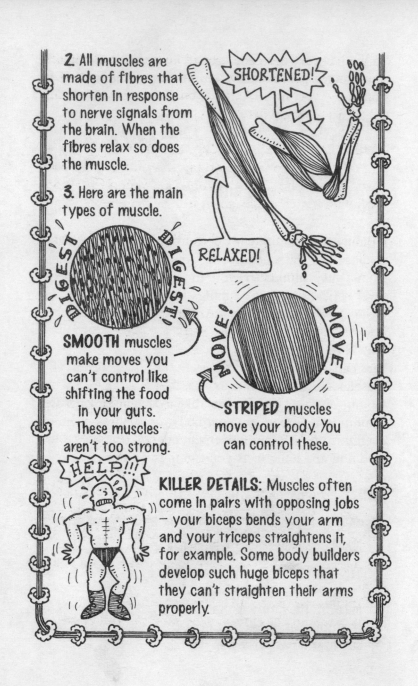

So you've got your head around how your body makes energy from mitochondria to muscles? Well, that's fab! Hopefully you've still got enough energy to try this rather exhausting quiz...

SEVEN SUPER-ENERGY QUIZ QUESTIONS

You should be able to race through this quiz because each question has just TWO possible answers. I just hope you're not in two minds about it!

1 Babies are more likely to have this than adults – what is it?

a) Built-in central heating.

b) Cold blood.

2 How much heat energy does your body give off when you're watching telly for an hour?

a) As much as an electric heater.

b) As much as a light bulb.

3 Which of these statements is correct?

a) Lazy people live longer than hard-working people because they use up less energy.

b) Hard work never killed anyone (as Dr Grimgrave likes to remind us).

GO ON, DOC – REMIND THEM!

HARD WORK NEVER KILLED ANYONE!

4 Why do children seem to have more energy than adults?

a) Children make energy faster than adults.

b) People of all ages produce the same amount of energy but adults prefer slobbing about.

5 Why do some people get overweight?

a) They eat more than they should.

b) Their bodies burn up food more slowly and spare food is stored as fat.

6 When does your brain use most energy?

a) In a science test.

b) When it's dreaming.

7 Why do people feel tired in the morning?

a) Their bodies are weak because they haven't eaten all night.

b) Their brains need glucose.

Answers:

1 a) Yes, babies really have central heating! They have a type of fat called brown fat (which adults have far less of). Mitochondria in the fat process fuel in a way that makes extra heat and this helps to keep the baby warm.

2 b) If you go for a run your body gives off the heat of ten light bulbs. In seven minutes of playing squash you can make enough heat to boil one litre of water.

3 b) Sorry, Harvey Tucker! Answer **a)** was suggested by US scientist Raymond Pearl (1879–1940) who wrote an article in 1927 entitled "Why lazy people live longest". But Pearl didn't take his own advice – he penned 700 articles and 17 books and he still lived to be 61.

4 a) Children's mitochondria are going at full blast making energy for an active lifestyle and a growing body. As a person gets older they slow down. And by the time they're as ancient as your more mature teachers, all their get up and go has got up and gone.

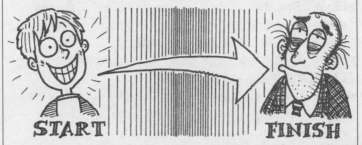

START   FINISH

5 a) Overweight people often make *more* energy than thinner people (it takes a lot of energy to shift a big body). The idea that overweight people don't eat too much comes from surveys where overweight people have fibbed about their eating habits. Now you might think that fat people eat more because they're greedy, but scientists have found that overweight people seem to take longer to feel full than thinner people.

6 b) If you fall asleep in your science test and start dreaming, your brain actually uses *more* energy than when you're awake! You may like to share this information with your teacher if she catches you sleeping during the test...

7 b) The brain needs glucose to make energy. Your blood contains just one hour's supply of glucose but your liver stores glucose in the form of a chemical called glycogen (gly-co-gen) to keep you going. But by morning your brain is hungry and it wants its glucose NOW! And that's why you feel tired and light-headed when you wake up. If you miss breakfast you might feel like a bike – two tyred to stand up – ha, ha.

TEACHER'S TEA-BREAK TEASER

At about 3 pm tap smartly on the staffroom door. When the door opens give your teacher a wide-awake smile and ask...

IS IT TRUE YOUR ENERGY LEVEL DROPS AT THIS TIME OF DAY?

MUMBLE, GROAN...

Answer:
Yes it does. Scientist Robert Thayer of the University of California interviewed lots of people.
Here's your teacher's day based on his findings...

DOZE!

7 am: Wake up feeling groggy...

SCIENCE, BLAH, BLAH, HOMEWORK, WITTER...

11 am: Energy levels have increased...

3 pm: Energy levels low...

7 pm: Energy levels pick up.

11 pm: Energy levels dipping to bed-time

Tired people tend to be more bad-tempered and the best treatment is exercise. In fact, I should have warned you earlier…

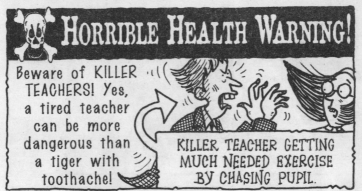

HORRIBLE HEALTH WARNING!

Beware of KILLER TEACHERS! Yes, a tired teacher can be more dangerous than a tiger with toothache!

KILLER TEACHER GETTING MUCH NEEDED EXERCISE BY CHASING PUPIL.

Of course your teacher may try to revive themselves with a nice hot mug of tea. But inside that mug of tea something interesting is going on. The heat is spreading – it's heating up the cup, it's warming your teacher … and eventually it'll warm up the rest of the universe.

What on Earth's going on…?

It's time to turn up the *heat*.

KILLER HEAT

Earlier we talked about cold (lack of heat energy) but now it's time for heat. Time for this book to warm up to its boiling, burning climax. Yes, it's time to get as hot as the hottest place in the universe!

But first a question to fire your imagination…

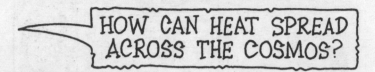

> HOW CAN HEAT SPREAD ACROSS THE COSMOS?

Whoops – that's a tricky one! We've asked Bernard Boyle back to answer your questions – let's hope he can keep his cool…

HORRIBLE SCIENCE QUESTION TIME

Today I'm going to tell you how heat energy spreads...

Is that "spreads" like margarine?

I expect that's 'eat energy.

Since heat is really just wobbling atoms it can spread from atom to atom as they knock into one another and start wobbling faster and faster. We scientists call this conduction (con-duck-shon).

A substance that allows heat to pass through it easily is called a good conductor — examples include metals.

My grandpa was a good conductor...

For heat?

No, the number 92 bus.

An insulator is a bad conductor. Examples include air, plastic and this rather trendy but sensible woolly jumper I'm wearing.

Heat can also spread through convection (con-veck-shon). That's the word for when hot air or water atoms' molecules move apart because they've got heat energy.

Why do they do that?

This makes the air or water lighter than the same amount of cold air or water. And so the hotter substance rises.

Shouldn't our teacher rise? He's full of hot air!

Finally, heat can spread through radiation.

RADIATION

Is that when people get zapped with high energy rays?

115

Well, yes but it's also a way that heat energy spreads in the form of a type of light that our eyes can't see. It's called infrared (in-fra-red) light.

INVISIBLE RAYS

It's what you're feeling when you feel hot in the sun. Now if you'll just turn to page 101 of my book...

That's right, INFRARED.

Did you say we're in for a read?

CONDUCTION IN ACTION

Conduction and insulation are so common I bet you come across them all the time. Yes, common as muck they are ... *and I can prove it!*

Bet you never knew!
Manure heaps steam in cold weather. The heat energy is actually made by billions of microbes cheerfully scoffing the delicious dung. But manure itself contains lots of air, water and bits of half-digested plants – all good insulators so that quite high temperatures can build up inside the heap until it's hot enough to steam. Fancy a steam in one?

Bet you never knew!

In the Second World War the Germans invaded Russia and in November 1941 they were poised to capture the Russian capital, Moscow. One night the temperature crashed. Thousands of soldiers were frost-bitten and their rotten feet had to be chopped off. The Germans wore boots shod with iron nails that conducted heat away from their feet. The Russians wore felt boots. Felt is a type of pressed wool. It's a good insulator and keeps the heat in. The Russians won and the Germans were left feeling sore about de-feet.

And talking about insulation...

Dare you discover ... what a sock does to ice?

You will need:

A sunny windowsill or bright lamp

Sock (it doesn't have to be clean but you may feel cheesed off if it smells)

Two ice cubes

Two saucers

Gloves to protect fingers from ice

What you do:

1 Put on gloves. Place one ice cube on one saucer.

2 Put the other ice cube in the sock and wrap the sock around it tightly. Place the sock on the second saucer.

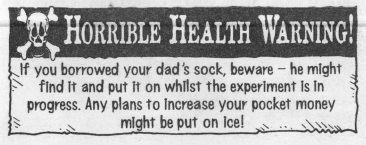

HORRIBLE HEALTH WARNING!

If you borrowed your dad's sock, beware – he might find it and put it on whilst the experiment is in progress. Any plans to increase your pocket money might be put on ice!

117

3 Place the ice cube and the sock 15 cm from the light bulb.

YOU MAY NEED BOOKS TO RAISE THE ICE TO THE RIGHT HEIGHT.

HMMM! I SMELL CHEESE!

4 Leave the experiment for 45 minutes.

What do you notice?
a) Both ice cubes have melted.
b) The ice cube in the saucer has melted but the ice cube in the sock hasn't.
c) The ice cube in the sock has melted but not the ice cube in the saucer.

Result
b) The ice cube in the sock should be only half-melted. Like any material, the sock is a good insulator – but if an object is already cold the insulator can keep it cold too! Here's what happened:

HEAT ENERGY

MOST HEAT ENERGY SOAKED UP BY SOCK, ICE STAYS COOL →

LAMP

INSULATED SNOW PERSON KEEPS COLD LONGER.

ANYONE SEEN MY JUMPER?

COULD YOU BE A SCIENTIST?

In 1960 the US Air Force carried out tests on volunteers to find out the greatest heat a human can survive. It turned out to be 260°C (500°F) – hotter than boiling water, hotter than a cooking steak. (I expect the volunteers were real hot-heads.) What were they wearing?

a) They were in the buff, raw, nip, nuddy or any other word that means that they wore no clothes.

b) A full set of clothing.

c) Flame proof underpants.

Answer:

b) A person can stand 60°C (140   ) *more* heat when wearing clothes because the clothing insulates the skin from the heat.

Bet you never knew!
At the World Sauna Championships in Finland people sit in a hot sauna room at temperatures up to 43°C (110°F) – this is as hot as some deserts! The aim is to sweat dirt from the skin but everyone wears swimming costumes because the organizers say it would be rude if they didn't.

Mind you, a heatwave can be as hot as a sauna. Killer heatwaves often strike the southern USA – in 1980, for example, thousands of people died as temperatures

119

soared above 37.7°C (100°F). In Dallas, Texas the official in charge of stopping cruelty to children said:

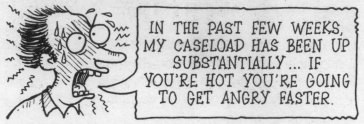

IN THE PAST FEW WEEKS, MY CASELOAD HAS BEEN UP SUBSTANTIALLY... IF YOU'RE HOT YOU'RE GOING TO GET ANGRY FASTER.

Yes, I'm sorry to say that hot-tempered parents were taking it out on their children. So, BE WARNED. It's not a smart idea to ask for extra pocket money when your dad's sweltering.

I'LL TAKE THAT AS A "NO", THEN

But, talking about heatwaves, there's one place where the weather is *always* boiling. It's one of the hottest places on Earth – it's so hot that the heat kills people *all the time*. One early visitor called it:

THE NEAREST TO A LITTLE HELL ON EARTH THAT THE WHOLE WICKED WORLD CAN PRODUCE.

It's California's Death Valley and *Living on the Edge Magazine* was after a fearless, super-fit, ultra-brave reporter to write a feature on the region. They couldn't find one, and so…

HARVEY TUCKER'S BIG ADVENTURE

I was summoned to the editor's office but I had my excuses ready.

"I can't go!" I moaned. "Please don't send me back to the Arctic I'll get hypo-what's it and lose all my toes!"

The editor folded her arms and shook her head.

"Cut the cackle, greedy-guts. You're not going to the Arctic and you won't get hypothermia. Sunstroke, sunburn, fever maybe, but no hypothermia!"

And she gave me my next assignment - a feature on the effects of heat in Death Valley. "Death Valley" — it's the kind of name that gives me a cold shiver — or should I say a hot shudder?

But as my old dad used to say, we Tuckers are like a bad pork pie - you can't keep us down! So I thought, "No sweat — I'll just go and check out the scenery," and I threw myself into planning. (Well, for five minutes — then I watched the game on TV.) Then I packed my sunnies, 26 tubes of sunblock, 15 jars of suncream, my laptop, a crate of cold drinks

121

and six family-sized boxes of ice-cream. That should keep me going! Then I dressed up in my home-made heat protection suit...

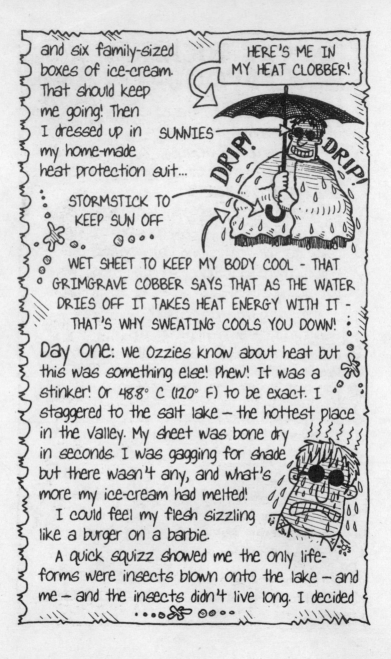

HERE'S ME IN MY HEAT CLOBBER!

SUNNIES

DRIP!

DRIP!

STORMSTICK TO KEEP SUN OFF

WET SHEET TO KEEP MY BODY COOL — THAT GRIMGRAVE COBBER SAYS THAT AS THE WATER DRIES OFF IT TAKES HEAT ENERGY WITH IT — THAT'S WHY SWEATING COOLS YOU DOWN!

Day One: We Ozzies know about heat but this was something else! Phew! It was a stinker! Or 48.8° C (120° F) to be exact. I staggered to the salt lake — the hottest place in the valley. My sheet was bone dry in seconds. I was gagging for shade but there wasn't any, and what's more my ice-cream had melted!

I could feel my flesh sizzling like a burger on a barbie.

A quick squizz showed me the only life-forms were insects blown onto the lake — and me — and the insects didn't live long. I decided

122

this place was real sticky — and so was I.
So I huddled under my stormstick and had a
go at some research. I downloaded some info
from the Internet — but my laptop melted! So
I took a gander at my book — maybe old Dr G
has something more to say about heat...

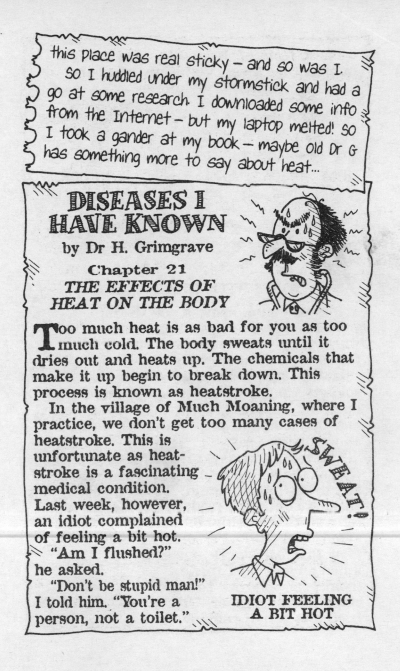

DISEASES I HAVE KNOWN

by Dr H. Grimgrave

Chapter 21
THE EFFECTS OF HEAT ON THE BODY

Too much heat is as bad for you as too much cold. The body sweats until it dries out and heats up. The chemicals that make it up begin to break down. This process is known as heatstroke.

In the village of Much Moaning, where I practice, we don't get too many cases of heatstroke. This is unfortunate as heatstroke is a fascinating medical condition. Last week, however, an idiot complained of feeling a bit hot.

"Am I flushed?" he asked.

"Don't be stupid man!" I told him. "You're a person, not a toilet."

SWEAT!

IDIOT FEELING A BIT HOT

123

The effects of heatstroke are easily summed up: fever, vomiting, headache, thirst, confusion, dry skin...

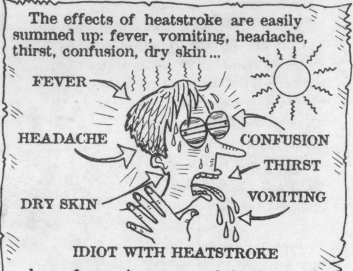

FEVER

HEADACHE

DRY SKIN

CONFUSION

THIRST

VOMITING

IDIOT WITH HEATSTROKE

...loss of consciousness and death.

So let that be a warming ... er ... *warning* to you. Sometimes the victim faints after feeling giddy.

In my days as an army doctor the soldiers would walk into lampposts during long, hot, marches. Their heart beat slowed and they couldn't pass water, or "urinate" as we doctors say.

The treatment is to rest in a cool place (I shut the soldiers in a cool food store) and drink lots of liquid. Water is the cheapest option, I find. Most doctors will tell you that victims of heatstroke should avoid hard work. Personally I take the view that hard work never killed anyone so I made them peel potatoes to make chips for my supper. It's a fried and tested remedy, ha ha.

"That's it" I thought "I'm crook, I've got heatstroke!" Just then I saw a sticky-beak scientist go swanning past – they study heat out here. She ordered me to drink 45 litres of water a day or my body would dry out! Too right – I was dripping with sweat. So I drank all my drinks – they were fizzy so I spent the next six hours burping.

BURP!

At last I found a motel with air-conditioning. Heaven!

I jumped into my cozzie and dived into the pool and stayed there until sunset with just my nose sticking out of the water.

Days 2-10

Still recovering so I spent the next few days bludging by the pool – the motel had a nice line in ice-cold lager, cold slushy milkshakes and 64 flavours of ice-cream – ace tucker! (I felt I ought to sample them all to decide which I liked best.) I was sure the magazine wouldn't go to the knuckle about the bill!

SLURP!

SOME HOT NEWS JUST IN...

The Earth is heating up and causing killer climate chaos. There have been deadly droughts and fatal floods and the woeful warmth is melting ice from the land and raising sea levels and causing more floods. And here's why...

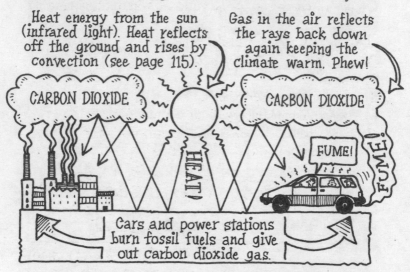

Heat energy from the sun (infrared light). Heat reflects off the ground and rises by convection (see page 115).

Gas in the air reflects the rays back down again keeping the climate warm. Phew!

CARBON DIOXIDE

CARBON DIOXIDE

HEAT!

FUME!

FUME!

Cars and power stations burn fossil fuels and give out carbon dioxide gas.

This is sometimes known as the "greenhouse effect" because the gas traps heat like the glass of a greenhouse. Okay – so any old science book will tell you this. But did you know that another gas causing global warming is methane? And a major cause of methane is farts – especially cows' farts (they blow-off more than humans) and also the farts of wood-eating insects called termites.

PARDON! FART! PARDON! FART! PARDON! FART! FART!

The greenhouse effect was discovered before it even became a problem. The possibility was pointed out by Irish scientist John Tyndall (1820–1895). Tyndall was a fantastic science teacher (yes, they do exist!). In one lecture at the Royal Institution in London he used the science of energy to play a cello ... without touching it!

COULD YOU BE A SCIENTIST?

OK, so how did he manage *that*?

Was it...

a) Energy from laser beams.

b) The movement energy of air blasting from an elephant's trunk.

c) Sound energy travelling along a pole from someone playing a piano in the basement.

Answer:
c) Sound energy passed along the pole and moved the cello's strings.

Sadly, Tyndall was poisoned accidentally by his wife when she gave him too much of the medicine he was taking.

Mind you, in the next chapter you'll find killer temperatures that make global warming seem a bit chilly. Can't you just hear the crackling and roaring from the next few fiery pages...

It's gonna be HOT.

Is the fire brigade ready?

FEARSOME FIERY FURNACES

Put heat energy into something and three things can happen.

1 If it's solid it might melt into a liquid like Harvey's ice cream and his laptop a few pages ago.

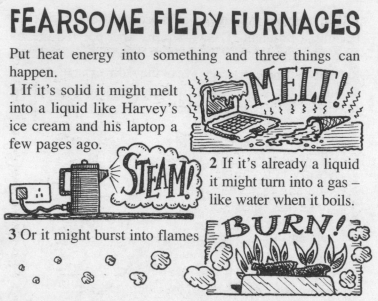

2 If it's already a liquid it might turn into a gas – like water when it boils.

3 Or it might burst into flames

Scientists call the first two effects a "change in state". Basically what's going on is that heat energy is making the atoms wobble so fast they break free of neighbouring atoms. If they stick close to their neighbours the substance is a liquid – but if they go off in search of adventure they're a gas.

ANXIOUS ATOMS

SHALL WE GO – OR SHALL WE STICK TOGETHER?

WANTED! ENERGETIC, ADVENTURE-SEEKING ATOMS. JOIN US – LIFE WILL BE A GAS!

Fire is different ... actually the posh scientific word is combustion (com-bust-tee-on).

Killer energy fact file

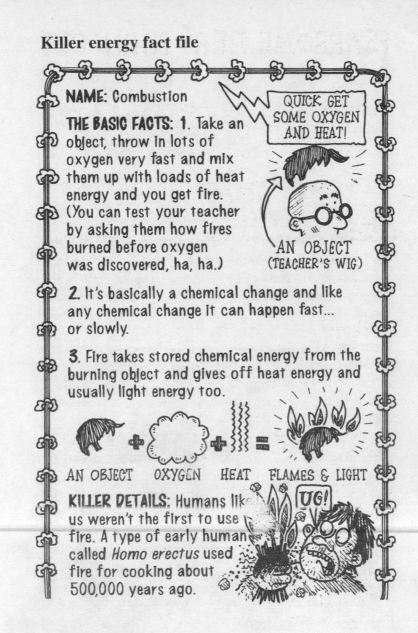

NAME: Combustion

THE BASIC FACTS: 1. Take an object, throw in lots of oxygen very fast and mix them up with loads of heat energy and you get fire. (You can test your teacher by asking them how fires burned before oxygen was discovered, ha, ha.)

QUICK GET SOME OXYGEN AND HEAT!

AN OBJECT (TEACHER'S WIG)

2. It's basically a chemical change and like any chemical change it can happen fast... or slowly.

3. Fire takes stored chemical energy from the burning object and gives off heat energy and usually light energy too.

AN OBJECT OXYGEN HEAT FLAMES & LIGHT

KILLER DETAILS: Humans like us weren't the first to use fire. A type of early human called *Homo erectus* used fire for cooking about 500,000 years ago.

UG!

Scientists have found traces of their fires near Beijing, China — so was this the first-ever Chinese takeaway? And ever since we've been finding horrible uses for fire...

SWEET AND SOUR MAMMOTH — FASCINATING!

FIVE FATAL FIERY FACTS...

1 Burning alive was the punishment in many countries for opposing the Church or being a witch – Gerolamo Cardano nearly suffered this fate – remember? If the executioner felt kind they might smear the victim's body with a kind of fast-burning tar called pitch to finish them off faster.

FANCY SOME PITCH?

TAR VERY MUCH!

2 In England women were burnt alive if they killed their husbands or clipped bits of silver off coins. The last woman to suffer this fate was Christian Murphy in 1789. A witness said

She behaved with great decency, but was most shocked at the dreadful punishment she was about to undergo.

No wonder she was shocked – if she'd been a man she'd have got off with a nice quick hanging.

3 Burning wasn't the only method in which fire helped to get rid of people. In ancient China criminals were fried in oil. The English King Henry VIII (1490–1547) ordered that people found guilty of poisoning should be boiled alive.

4 Archaeologists have studied skeletons from Herculaneum, a Roman town destroyed by a volcano in AD 79. The people had been killed by superheated gases and the archaeologists found that their brains had boiled whilst they were *still alive*.

5 People who think that humans can burst into flames for unknown reasons (this is called spontaneous human combustion) have blamed the mystery fires on fart gases such as methane that burn easily. Scientists explain this burning question in terms of sparks from static electricity but either way it must be a nasty way to glow, er, go.

And now for more burning questions...

COULD YOU BE A SCIENTIST?

The human body burns at around 600–950°C (1112–1710°F) but some victims of spontaneous human combustion have been found burnt to ashes leaving their surroundings untouched.

How is this possible?

a) The fire was hot and quick-burning and burnt itself out.

b) The fire made the bodies explode from inside.

c) The fire burned like a candle, consuming the body's fat at high temperatures, but it didn't spread.

Answer:
c) Non-fatty bits like the legs are often left amongst the ashes. In 1986 a scientist from Leeds University, England, set fire to a dead pig to produce similar results. Crispy bacon, anyone?

Bet you never knew!
It was once thought the victims were drunken people and the fires were made hot by alcohol burning inside them. So scientist Justus von Liebig (remember him from page 102) tried soaking bits of dead body in alcohol and setting them on fire. They didn't burn. He then got rats drunk and set them on fire but they didn't burn either.

☠ HORRIBLE HEALTH WARNING!

Getting your pet hamster drunk and setting it on fire is extremely cruel and dangerous. Anyone who tries this experiment may find themselves locked away until they are no longer a menace to hamsters. *Hic!*

COULD YOU BE A SCIENTIST?

In the Pacific Islands, India, Japan, Greece and many other parts of the world people do fire walking. They walk across glowing embers at 649°C (1200°F) in their *bare feet* without scorching their clothes or burning their feet.

How is this possible?

a) It's all to do with the conduction of heat.

b) They have flame-proof skin on their feet.

c) They're protected by magical charms.

Answer:

a) The embers are carbon or stones which are poor conductors of heat. This slows the speed at which the heat gets to a walker's feet. The feet themselves are wet or sweaty and this also slows the heat. And the walkers usually move too quickly for their feet to burn. Mind you, it's still a brave feet ... er ... *feat*.

☠ HORRIBLE HEALTH WARNING!

Don't try anything like this – you might not be so lucky.

But talking about burning bodies – having recovered from his ordeal in Death Valley, Harvey Tucker is now facing his sternest challenge yet ... can he stand the *heat*?

HARVEY TUCKER'S BIG ADVENTURE

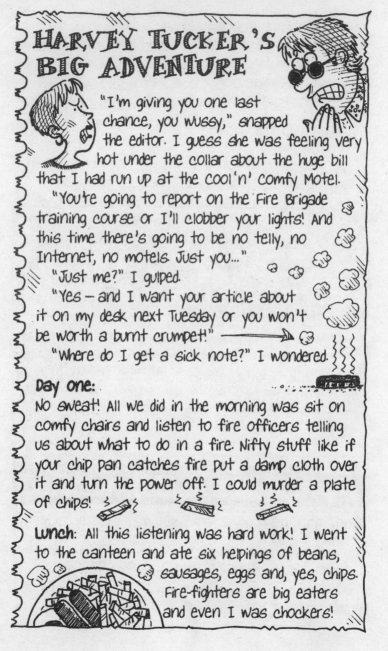

"I'm giving you one last chance, you wussy," snapped the editor. I guess she was feeling very hot under the collar about the huge bill that I had run up at the Cool 'n' Comfy Motel.

"You're going to report on the Fire Brigade training course or I'll clobber your lights! And this time there's going to be no telly, no Internet, no motels. Just you..."

"Just me?" I gulped.

"Yes – and I want your article about it on my desk next Tuesday or you won't be worth a burnt crumpet!" ⟶

"Where do I get a sick note?" I wondered.

Day one:

No sweat! All we did in the morning was sit on comfy chairs and listen to fire officers telling us about what to do in a fire. Nifty stuff like if your chip pan catches fire put a damp cloth over it and turn the power off. I could murder a plate of chips!

Lunch:

All this listening was hard work! I went to the canteen and ate six helpings of beans, sausages, eggs and, yes, chips. Fire-fighters are big eaters and even I was chockers!

134

Afternoon: Things got queasy in the arvo. The Fire Officer started blathering about burns and scalds. You've got to rinse them under cold running water and get medical advice if they're bad. Then he showed gross piccies of burn injuries. They're worse if the burn goes though the skin so there's no skin left. Also the heart and kidneys can shut down as blood moves towards the wound.

Then we looked at piccies of burned dead bods. Well, everyone else did – I covered my eyes. If you carry a burnt bod the guts can fall out and the arms and legs drop off.

I needed some air.

I took a dekko at the canteen to check out the tucker – sausages again. I left in a hurry clutching my mouth – I felt fit to chunder!

"Well, Harvey mate," I thought, "this is as bad as it gets."

I was wrong...

The Fire Officer announced that tomorrow we'd be tested on how to survive in a real burning building!!! What a choice – if I stuck the course I might catch fire – if I didn't I'd be fired anyway!

Day 2

The day started bad and that was the best bit...

"The main danger," said the Fire Officer, "is flashover or backdraft. Imagine an explosion of heat at 1000° C (1832° F). It's hot enough to burn the clothes off your back and split your bones open. It's so hot that even a jet of water from a hose turns to steam."

I imagined it – and closed my eyes and tried to think of food. This usually calms me down but for some reason I started thinking about flaming Xmas puds!

After a real 'mis' hour of waiting and ten visits to the dunny it was my turn. At the training school they have a real-sized building that they stage training fires in. I found myself in the bedroom...

"Close the door!" yelled the Fire Officer through his megaphone.

I did as I was told but smoke began to ooze under the door.

"Block the gap with a wet towel!" he instructed. I found a towel – it was dry so I called for help.

"There's a tap in the basin!"

"I can't see it – there's too much smoke!" I yelled.

HELP!

It's true I couldn't even see my fingers. But then I found the tap – I wet the towel and stuffed it under the door. Then I wet myself – with water from the tap, you'll understand. I thought it might stop me bursting into flames.

SPLASH! "Get out of the building, Tucker!" barked the Fire Officer.

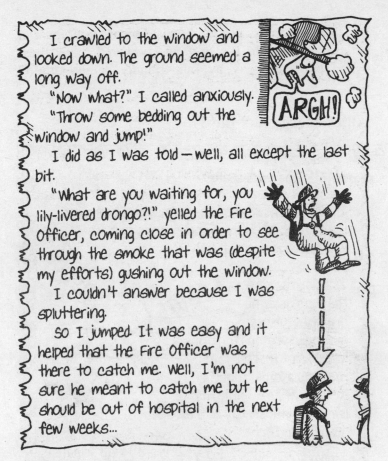

I crawled to the window and looked down. The ground seemed a long way off.

"Now what?" I called anxiously.

"Throw some bedding out the window and jump!"

I did as I was told — well, all except the last bit.

"What are you waiting for, you lily-livered drongo?!" yelled the Fire Officer, coming close in order to see through the smoke that was (despite my efforts) gushing out the window.

I couldn't answer because I was spluttering.

So I jumped. It was easy and it helped that the Fire Officer was there to catch me. Well, I'm not sure he meant to catch me but he should be out of hospital in the next few weeks...

ARGH!

GETTING HOTTER...

If there's one thing worse than a flashover, it's a firestorm. A huge killer fire that sucks air from its surroundings in hurricane force gusts and sucks in humans too. Temperatures can reach 800°C (1,472°F) – hot enough to melt glass and lead. And the heat is enough to spread the fire as houses nearby get so hot they burst into flames. And the fire consumes all the air in the area and kills anyone who isn't burnt to death.

But the firestorm is not the hottest temperature you can get by any stretch. It's *nothing* compared to the heat belted out every day by our friendly neighbourhood star...

Killer energy fact file

NAME: The sun's energy

THE BASIC FACTS 1. The sun's super-hot core is about 15 MILLION°C and even its surface is a rather sweaty 5,500°C.

2. Inside the core the sun's gigantic gravity squishes hydrogen protons (protons = specks of matter that make up atoms) together to form helium. Some matter is turned into energy and escapes as heat and light.

LIGHT! HEAT!

100,000,000°C! PHEW! THINK I'LL TAKE MY JACKET OFF...

LAB

300,000,000°C! SWEAT! I'LL TAKE MY SHIRT OFF...

LAB

3. In 1994 US scientists used the same process to heat atoms to 510 MILLION°C. But that's nothing. In 2006 US scientists used an X-ray blasting machine to cook tungsten atoms

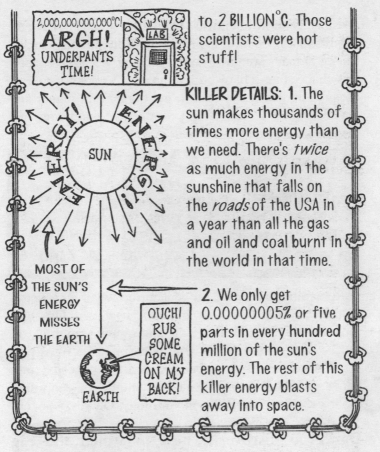

to 2 BILLION°C. Those scientists were hot stuff!

KILLER DETAILS: 1. The sun makes thousands of times more energy than we need. There's *twice* as much energy in the sunshine that falls on the *roads* of the USA in a year than all the gas and oil and coal burnt in the world in that time.

2. We only get 0.00000005% or five parts in every hundred million of the sun's energy. The rest of this killer energy blasts away into space.

THE SUN SOUNDS PRETTY AWESOME – DOESN'T IT?

Well, it's nothing special. Just an average star amongst 100,000,000,000 (100 billion) others in an average galaxy amongst 100 billion other galaxies in the known universe. For REAL energy you need to go back to the Big Bang. That's the start of the universe about 15 billion years ago.

All the energy in the universe was stuffed into a tiny dot smaller than an atom. And it was so hot no one can possibly say how hot it was. Even after it had cooled a bit it was still 10,000 million million million million degrees. Lucky humans weren't around then or we'd have stood less chance than a baby budgie on a cat's cookery course. Meanwhile this dot started to get bigger and bigger and BIGGER and it still hasn't stopped ... and now it's the universe!

LIFE-SIZE SKETCH OF UNIVERSE DURING THE BIG BANG

Remember the First Law of Thermodynamics? It says that energy can't be lost but that heat can turn into movement energy. Well, all the energy you can think of, all the energy of animals and electricity, the energy in your muscles and your beating heart, first came into being with the Big Bang. And every night you can watch the traces of the Big Bang on your telly. Oh yes, you can!

Dare you discover ... how to watch the Big Bang on TV?

You will need:
A TV
What you do:
1 Switch on the TV.
2 Switch it to a channel that hasn't been tuned in to any station.

What do you notice?
a) The screen shows strange alien forms.

b) There are hundreds of little dots of light dancing around.
c) There are strange patterns that look like explosions.

Answer:
b) The dots are made by microwaves – yes, the same type of energy that would zap the milky bar in a microwave oven – but these microwaves have been around since the Big Bang.
The microwaves are the last lingering echoes of that gigantic energy drifting for ever through the cold empty darkness of space. And they're far more interesting than some TV programmes I could mention.
And so we end this chapter with...

Didn't you say on page 8 that you were going to tell us the fate of the universe?

THAT VERY ALERT READER FROM PAGE 92

Oh, I'm sorry it must have slipped my mind! Well, it's just a small detail but the ultimate fate of the universe is...

OOPS – sorry readers we seem to have run out of space for this chapter – you'll have to read on to find out...

A POWER FOR GOOD?

Energy is everywhere – in the singing of the birds and the swaying of the grass. It makes us warm and comfortable and it's the killer monster in a raging fire. It's in turning the pages of this book and every wisp of steam from a kettle. Energy is the pulse of the universe and without it the universe would die.

The Big Bang and the Laws of Thermodynamics supply clues about the future. In particular there's a miserable message in the Second Law – yes, the one about heat energy always being lost. Here's how Scottish scientist James Clerk Maxwell (1831–1879) summed it up:

If you throw a tumblerful of water into the sea you cannot get the same tumbler of water back again.

Sounds reasonable – and if you don't believe me you can always try it next time you're at the seaside…

WHERE'S MY DRINK?

What Maxwell was saying was that the amount of confusion and muddle in the universe is always growing.

It's like drops of water mixing in the sea and it'll *never* sort itself out on its own. It makes sense. Think of your bedroom – I bet you it *never* tidies itself on its own!

Now look at energy. The universe started off as a tidy little dot of energy all squashed neatly in one place. But now it's an untidy hotch-potch of hot stars and cold space and it's getting worse. The Second Law says that energy is always getting lost in the form of heat energy. So where does all this heat energy go? Well, the Second Law has the answer: heat always heads for the coldest place it can find – and that, ultimately, is outer space.

And once heat energy drifts off into space no one can ever get it back – never, ever, ever. And that means one day all the energy in the universe will have turned to heat and floated off into space. The stars will sputter out like candle flames and the planets will die of cold. Eventually even the dusty remains of the stars and planets will turn to heat energy and drift away.

The universe will be a thin cold soup of tiny bits of atoms floating about in the dark emptiness. Time will go on but nothing will ever change, and nothing will ever happen again. It'll be worse than a wet winter weekend when the telly's broken down.

SPOT THE DIFFERENCE COMPETITION

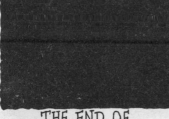

THE END OF
THE UNIVERSE

SCIENCE CLASS WITH
THE LIGHTS OFF

And in the end the loss of its energy will kill the universe – if it doesn't die of boredom first!

But let's look on the bright side. For one thing, it's not going to happen before the weekend. Scientists think it will take about 1,000,000,000,000,000,000,000,000,000,000 (one thousand billion billion billion) years. And they've got plenty of time to find a way to get the heat energy back or perhaps find a nice new universe for us to live in.

Or we might discover a new kind of power. People who believe that UFOs are alien spacecraft claim that they might work through some kind of anti-gravity force. This would have to get its energy from somewhere, and perhaps one day we'll find out...

Bet you never knew!
In 1878 inventor Thomas Edison (1847–1931) wanted to invent anti-gravity underwear that floated around in mid-air! A drawing of the time shows a dad towing his floating children.

But wait, would YOU fancy turning up at school in a pair of ground-defying knickers?

More urgently (and seriously) we're still running out of oil and gas energy and cooking our planet with the greenhouse effect. As usual, scientists are thinking up lots of answers, but whatever is done it's bound to involve developing renewable forms of energy like the sun's power and geothermal, wind and wave energy. These aren't going to run out like fossil fuels and don't give off gases that cause global warming.

But as the world fills up with people and more people travel in space we're going to need lots more energy. So here are some possibilities for the future...

SUPER-SUN SATELLITE SOARS!

Scientists are thrilled at the success of a giant satellite going round the sun. The satellite picks up power and beams it to Earth in the form of microwave rays. Said one beaming boffin, "We've taken a real shine to this project!"

POO POWERS PLANET PROBE!

It was revealed today that the interplanetary spacecraft is powered by fuel cells fuelled by germs eating rotting astronauts' poo.

Scientists in Michigan State University, USA began working on this project in 2000. A scientist said, "We thought the idea stinks – but it's proved to be out of this world."

SUPER-CELL SPARS SPEED-SPURT!

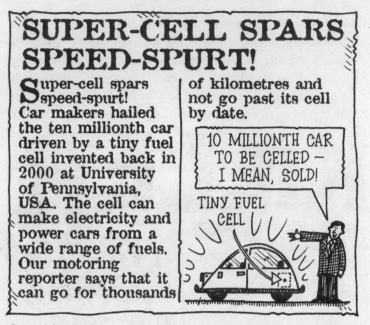

Super-cell spars speed-spurt! Car makers hailed the ten millionth car driven by a tiny fuel cell invented back in 2000 at University of Pennsylvania, USA. The cell can make electricity and power cars from a wide range of fuels. Our motoring reporter says that it can go for thousands of kilometres and not go past its cell by date.

10 MILLIONTH CAR TO BE CELLED — I MEAN, SOLD!

TINY FUEL CELL

One thing's for sure: science has come a long way in understanding energy. And perhaps one day human cleverness will find a way of turning killer energy into a power for good.

I'LL DRINK TO THAT!

KILLER ENERGY

QUIZ

Now find out if you're a
Killer Energy expert!

Are you feeling energized? Plug in the power, crank up the grey matter, and have a go at these awesome energy quizzes to find out.

Energy in everything

Energy is everywhere, changing from one form to another, but have you got to grips with all the different types? Match the freakish forms of energy below with their strange sources.

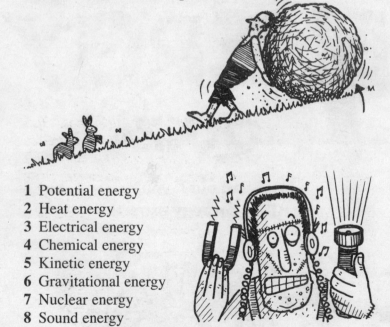

1 Potential energy
2 Heat energy
3 Electrical energy
4 Chemical energy
5 Kinetic energy
6 Gravitational energy
7 Nuclear energy
8 Sound energy

a) The energy you generate when you're snoring in your Horrible Science lesson
b) The energy that causes lightning during a storm

c) The energy in use when you're riding your bike

d) The energy at work when you fall off your bike...

e) The energy packed into your banana and peanut butter sandwich

f) The energy in the stretched elastic band just before you flick it at your teacher

g) The energy created when atoms bash into each other at supersonic speeds

h) The energy you lose in sweat when you run for the bus

Answers:
1f; 2h; 3b; 4e; 5c; 6d; 7g; 8a

Fantastic fuel

Without fuel life would be very different. You wouldn't be able to watch boring TV documentaries with your mum and dad. The dentist's drill wouldn't work. You wouldn't be able to get to your Horrible Science lessons on time by driving to school. But if you think life would be more fun without fuel, take this quick quiz and think again...

1 We rely on fossil fuels for millions of everyday things, but which of the following is a fossil fuel?
a) The sun
b) Natural gas
c) Cow poo

2 ATP is the type of chemical fuel your body stores in case you want to move from the sofa to the kitchen to raid the biscuit tin. But what does ATP stand for?
a) Adenoidal Tuppawareplate
b) Adenosine Triphosphate
c) Add The Power

3 How many elephants could be lifted 1 metre in the air by the power of 1 kg of awesome uranium atoms?
a) 200 million
b) 200
c) 2 (and baby ones at that)

4 A French cement company found a way of using radical recycling in their processes. What is the fantastic new fuel they're using to fire their kilns?
a) Used nappies
b) Used toilet paper
c) Snotty tissues

5 Which curious chemical fuel is stored on the side of matchboxes and combines with the air to burn brightly but briefly when struck?

a) Oxygen
b) Gold
c) Phosphorus

6 Which type of radical renewable fuel is pumped from the ground and uses the heat from masses of molten rocks below the Earth's surface?
a) Hydroelectric
b) Geothermal
c) Methane

7 What sweet ingredient can be used to make the biofuel ethanol?
a) Sugar cane
b) Candy floss
c) Honey

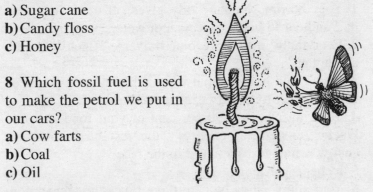

8 Which fossil fuel is used to make the petrol we put in our cars?
a) Cow farts
b) Coal
c) Oil

Answers:
1b; 2b; 3a; 4a; 5c; 6b; 7a; 8c

Horrible heat and killer cold

Strange scientists spent years figuring out how heat and cold affect things. They came up with some crazy ideas along the way – and some unbelievable discoveries. Can you figure out if these fascinating facts are the chilling truth or just a lot of hot air?

1 Your horrible human body gives off enough heat in half an hour to boil a saucepan of water.

2 Everything in the awesome universe is getting hotter and hotter.

3 It's so cold in space that when astronaut pee is ejected from a rocket toilet it freezes immediately.

4 Your muscles turn 90 per cent of your food fuel into kinetic (movement) energy – the rest turns into heat energy, which turns you red in the face.

5 Icebergs can sing.

6 Your slimy saliva boils at three times the temperature of ordinary water.

7 You'll almost certainly catch a cold if you spend too long in the snow.

8 Goose bumps are your body's way of warming up.

Answers:
1 TRUE. Who needs electricity to make a cuppa when you can just cuddle the kettle?

2 FALSE. Everything is constantly losing heat. To keep things toasty you have to add heat energy.

3 TRUE. That's a *wee* bit of space trivia for you…

4 FALSE. Only a quarter is used to make you motor, all the rest is sticky sweat.

5 TRUE. They probably wouldn't get far on X-factor, but the noise they make when they grind together is a bit like a cool chorus.

6 TRUE. Don't try sticking your tongue in a saucepan though.

7 FALSE. Extreme cold *kills* germs, so you won't suffer from sniffles at the South Pole.

8 TRUE. Goose bumps make your hairs stand on end, which helps trap your body heat.

Meet the scientists

Over the centuries scientists have carried out many amazing energy experiments and have blown hot and cold over the laws of thermodynamics. Sometimes they got it right – and sometimes they got it really wrong. From the clues below, can you match the brilliant brainbox with his discovery?

1 Noticing a cannon heating up while being bored by a drill, this stunning scientist realized that heat wasn't a substance – it was energy caused by the rubbing of the drill (sadly, everyone thought his discovery was boring!)

2 A lot of hot air drove this impatient inventor to figure out how to use steam to pump water from mines (he was *steaming* drunk when he made the discovery).

3 An amusing accident with a teapot resulted in this strange Scottish scientist discovering that burning coal released a gas that could be used to produce heat and light energy (it certainly *fuelled* his imagination as an inventor).

4 This German genius of a doctor made the stupendous discovery that stuffing your face with food gave you enough energy to move (it was *bleeding* obvious, really).

5 We remember this fancy physicist by the temperature scale that bears his name. He discovered how cold it had to be to freeze water, and how hot the human body was (although he got that last bit wrong).

6 This amazing mathematician calculated that nothing can be chillier than absolute zero. For being so brilliantly bright, he was allowed to put his name to another scientific scale (pretty cool, huh?).

7 By using steam to turn a turbine, this Irish inventor sent ships speeding round the seas (it *revolutionized* the energy industry).

8 This Swedish inventor made an illuminating discovery – he figured out to use the stored energy in phosphorus to light up a match (he really was a bright *spark*).

a) William Thomson, Lord Kelvin
b) Charles Parsons
c) Benjamin Thompson, Count Rumford
d) Daniel Fahrenheit
e) John Lundstrom
f) William Murdock
g) Julius Robert von Mayer
h) Thomas Savery

Answers:
1c; 2h; 3f; 4g; 5d; 6a; 7b; 8e

Confusing renewable energy

From deep underground and high in the sky, nature has provided the means to generate amazing energy in ways that might save our precarious planet. Untangle these energy anagrams to identify the fantastic renewable phrases.

1 PEARL SALON (2 words)

CLUE: Put one of these on the roof of your house to harness the heat of the super sun.

2 GAMER HOTEL (1 word)

CLUE: This type of energy bubbles and burps its way up from deep within the Earth.

3 UNBID WINTER (2 words)

CLUE: The air causes this incredible invention to twist and turn and generate electricity.

4 CLEAR INFUSIONS (2 words)

CLUE: This powerful process uses energy from atoms in a chain reaction.

5 CORRECTLY HID YETI (1 word)

CLUE: The power of running water makes this type of amazing energy.

6 WEAVE PROW (2 words)

CLUE: You'll see that the sea plays a big part in creating this energy.

7 LEADING TYRE (2 words)

CLUE: The effects of the moon help with this watery renewable power source.

8 BOIL FUSE (1 word)

CLUE: Stuffing the tank of your car with sugar, perhaps?

Answers:

1 Solar panel
2 Geothermal
3 Wind turbine
4 Nuclear fission
5 Hydroelectricity
6 Wave power
7 Tidal energy
8 Biofuels

HORRIBLE INDEX

161

SHOCKING ELECTRICITY

INTRODUCTION

Phew! It's the end of another day...

Mind you, science is boring – especially the science of electricity. That's SHOCKINGLY boring. So the alien monster probably got bored out of its two tentacle brains.

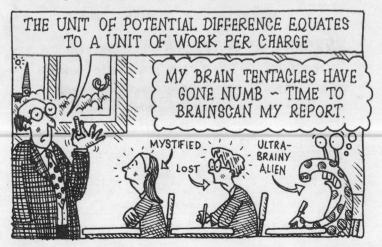

Oddbl⊗b the Blurb

► **STAR-DATE:** Present

MISSION: Observation of humanoid activity on planet known as "Earth".

GALAXY CO-ORDINATES:
0001.1100.0011100.0

BACKGROUND: Juvenile humanoids or "children" are subjected to factual information by adult humanoids at a gathering known as a "science lesson". Tests reveal that 99 per cent of data is forgotten by the children. This can result in a primitive display of aggression by the adult humanoid.

J.H.

A.H.

PRESENT ACTIVITY: Monitoring of "science lesson" in a primitive shelter known as a "school".

BRAINSCAN VIDEO

TODAY'S TOPIC IS ELECTRICITY

DRIBBLE! DOZE! YAWN!

NOTES: Juvenile humanoids enter an altered state of awareness known as "snoozing".

Are your science lessons this bad? Does learning about electricity leave you in shock? Well, if science makes you suffer then reading this book could change your life. These pages are buzzing with shocking facts about electricity and humming with shocking stories including: the scientist who got struck by lightning, the surgeon who gave an electric shock to a gory human heart and the scientist who had a man *killed* to win an argument. After all, who needs *boring* science when you can have HORRIBLE Science?!

So what are you waiting for? Why not plug in and switch over to the next page!

SHOCKING ELECTRICAL POWER

This book is guaranteed free from electrical failure. Er – well, that's probably because it doesn't run on electricity unlike lots of other things – like toasters and televisions and fans and fridges. Where would we be without electricity? Well, you could be on a HORRIBLE SCIENCE HOLIDAY – just take a look at this:

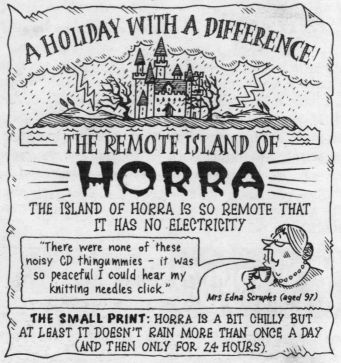

A HOLIDAY WITH A DIFFERENCE!

THE REMOTE ISLAND OF

HORRA

THE ISLAND OF HORRA IS SO REMOTE THAT
IT HAS NO ELECTRICITY

"There were none of these noisy CD thingummies – it was so peaceful I could hear my knitting needles click."

Mrs Edna Scruples (aged 97)

THE SMALL PRINT: HORRA IS A BIT CHILLY BUT AT LEAST IT DOESN'T RAIN MORE THAN ONCE A DAY (AND THEN ONLY FOR 24 HOURS).

So you don't fancy a bit of Horra? Well *tough* – it looks like you and your whole class are going there anyway – on a field trip.

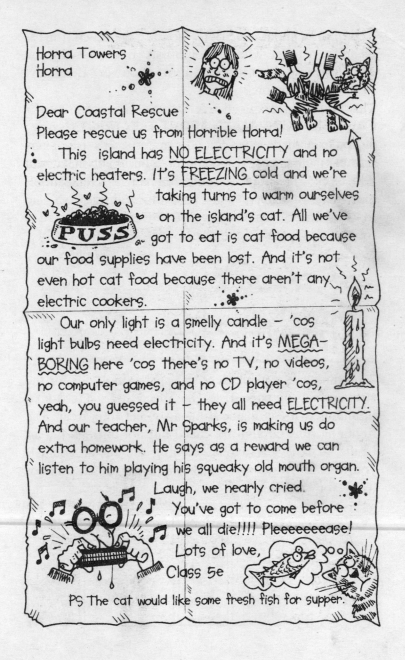

Horra Towers
Horra

Dear Coastal Rescue
Please rescue us from Horrible Horra!
This island has <u>NO ELECTRICITY</u> and no electric heaters. It's <u>FREEZING</u> cold and we're taking turns to warm ourselves on the island's cat. All we've got to eat is cat food because our food supplies have been lost. And it's not even hot cat food because there aren't any electric cookers.

Our only light is a smelly candle — 'cos light bulbs need electricity. And it's <u>MEGA-BORING</u> here 'cos there's no TV, no videos, no computer games, and no CD player 'cos, yeah, you guessed it — they all need <u>ELECTRICITY</u>. And our teacher, Mr Sparks, is making us do extra homework. He says as a reward we can listen to him playing his squeaky old mouth organ. Laugh, we nearly cried.
You've got to come before we all die!!!! Pleeeeeeease!
Lots of love,
Class 5e

PS The cat would like some fresh fish for supper.

169

Yep, life without electricity sounds as much fun as cleaning a toilet with a toothbrush. But what do you actually know about this vital form of power? Heard any of these facts before?

FOUR SHOCKING FACTS ABOUT ELECTRICITY

1 You can make electricity from farts. It's true – by burning methane gas (found in some farts) you make heat which can be used to power generators and make electricity. Methane is also found in rotting rubbish, and in the United States there are 100 power stations based at rubbish tips that burn the gas.

2 Lightning is a giant electrical spark (look out for the striking facts on page 218). One place that's safe from a lightning strike is inside a metal object like a car. The lightning runs through the metal but not through the air inside – so if you avoid touching the metal yourself you're safe. Much safer than sheltering in an outdoor toilet, for example.

3 Sometimes electrical power can surge when the power station pumps out too much electricity. (Imagine a huge wave of power surging into your sockets.) In 1990 people in the English village of Piddlehinton (yes, that's the name) were shocked when a power surge blew up their cookers and TVs.

4 The biggest power cut in history hit the north-east United States and Ontario, Canada in 1965. Thirty million people were plunged into darkness, but luckily only two were killed in the confusion.

Now you can test your knowledge further in this quickie quiz. It's bound to spark your interest.

SHOCKING QUIZ
1 Which of these machines *doesn't* need electricity to work?
a) The toilet
b) The telephone
c) The radio

2 Why is it that the victim of a huge electric shock gets thrown through the air? (No need to test this on family pets or frail elderly teachers.)
a) The force of the electricity lifts them off the ground.
b) The electric current runs through the nerves and

makes the muscles jerk violently so the victim leaps backwards.

c) Electricity reverses the force of gravity and makes the body weightless for a second.

3 Your teacher gets struck by lightning in the playground during a storm. Why is it dangerous to be in the playground at the same time?

a) You might have to give your teacher the kiss of life.

b) The playground will be wet from rain. The electric current from the lightning can spread through the wet surface and give you a nasty shock.

c) The hot lightning turns playground puddles into dangerous super-heated steam.

Answers:
1 a) Even if the radio doesn't work off mains electricity it will be powered by electricity from a battery. When you're chatting on the phone to a friend the receiver turns your voice into electric signals that travel down the wire to your friend's phone where they're changed into sounds again. Got all that? Toilets aren't powered by electricity but you may be interested to know that in 1966 inventor Thomas J Bayard devised an electrically powered wobbling toilet seat. The idea was that pummelling the bum prevents constipation.

Sadly, people poo-poohed the idea and the seat went off the market.

2 b) This is handy because the person is usually thrown a safe distance from the object that's giving them the shock. Another effect of a violent shock to the muscles and nerves is to make you poo and pee ... resulting in shockingly smelly underwear.

3 b) Electricity can pass through water – which is why it is extremely silly to put any electrical machine (not designed for it) near water or to touch power sockets or switches with wet fingers.

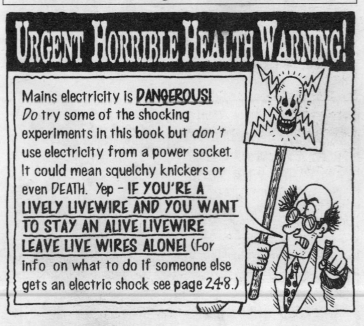

URGENT HORRIBLE HEALTH WARNING!

Mains electricity is **DANGEROUS!** *Do* try some of the shocking experiments in this book but *don't* use electricity from a power socket. It could mean squelchy knickers or even DEATH. Yep – **IF YOU'RE A LIVELY LIVEWIRE AND YOU WANT TO STAY AN ALIVE LIVEWIRE LEAVE LIVE WIRES ALONE!** (For info on what to do if someone else gets an electric shock see page 248.)

But before you get stuck into those experiments here's an important and interesting question: What on Earth is electricity actually *made of*? If you don't know read on – the answer's in the next shocking chapter!

SHOCKING ELECTRICAL SECRETS

OK, so what *is* electricity made of? Hands up who knows…

Oh dear, it looks like Mr Sparks, the science teacher, knows the answer:

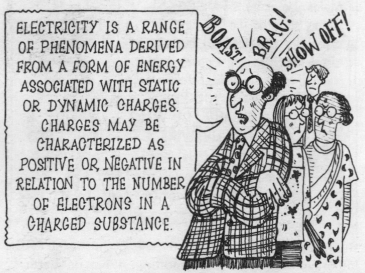

Well, thank you, Mr Sparks. Anyone understand that?

No? OK, let's try again. Everything in the universe is made of titchy bits called atoms and most atoms are surrounded by a cloud of even smaller blips of energy called electrons.

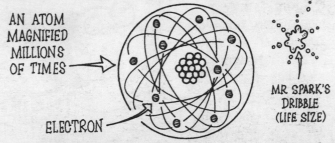

AN ATOM
MAGNIFIED
MILLIONS
OF TIMES →

ELECTRON

MR SPARK'S
DRIBBLE
(LIFE SIZE)

The electricity in your power sockets is actually *made of* moving electrons and the *power* of electricity comes from the force the electrons give out.

Let's imagine an atom as a family...

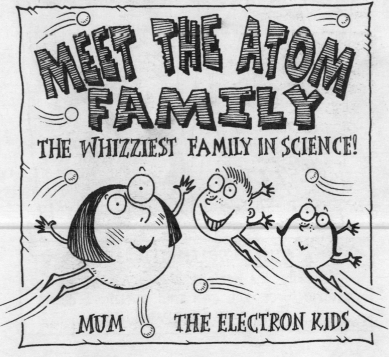

MEET THE ATOM FAMILY

THE WHIZZIEST FAMILY IN SCIENCE!

MUM   THE ELECTRON KIDS

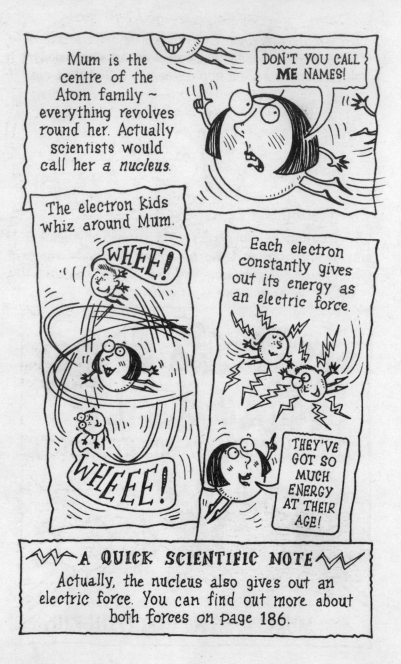

Electrons really are tiny. An electron is ten thousand times smaller than the nucleus. If you had a very steady hand you could put 1,000,000,000,000 (one thousand billion) electrons in a line and even then you wouldn't have quite enough to stretch across a pinhead!

IT'S A
WOBBLY
LINE, SMITH.
START AGAIN

IT'S A NUMBERS GAME

- Got a torch? All right then, switch it on and start counting – 1, 2, 3...

- That dim feeble light in your torch bulb uses 6,280,000,000,000,000,000 – (6.28 billion billion) electrons *every second*. Just to give you some idea of how massive this number is...

- A school day has about 23,400 seconds – if you don't believe me try counting them! So if you wanted to get to a million you'd have to count non-stop for another ten days.

...EIGHT HUNDRED
AND SEVENTY TWO
THOUSAND, THREE
HUNDRED AND
NINETY ONE...

- If you kept counting for another 32 years and 354 days (and that means counting whilst eating and

177

sleeping and going to the toilet) you'd eventually reach one billion (if you hadn't died of boredom).

- Not gobsmacked yet? Well, get this... In order to count those electrons used by your dim and feeble little torch *in just one second* you should have started counting well before the Earth was formed 4,600 million years ago!

A NOTE TO THE READER...

What we call an "electric current" is actually a stream of electrons flowing through a wire – this is measured in amps. Can you imagine what it would be like to *swim* in this stream? Here's a story about a person who did just that. He's an odd-job worker called Andy Mann – good name, eh? It all began when Andy got a shrinking feeling and was made to feel very very small...

178

IT'S A SMALL, SMALL, SMALL, SMALL WORLD

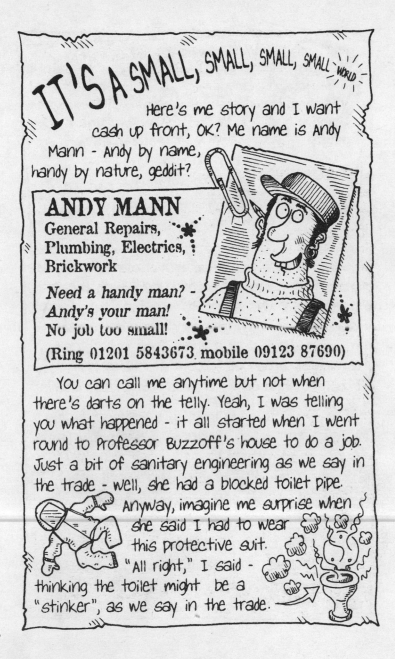

Here's me story and I want cash up front, OK? Me name is Andy Mann - Andy by name, handy by nature, geddit?

ANDY MANN
General Repairs,
Plumbing, Electrics,
Brickwork

Need a handy man? -
Andy's your man!
No job too small!

(Ring 01201 5843673 mobile 09123 87690)

You can call me anytime but not when there's darts on the telly. Yeah, I was telling you what happened - it all started when I went round to Professor Buzzoff's house to do a job. Just a bit of sanitary engineering as we say in the trade - well, she had a blocked toilet pipe.

Anyway, imagine me surprise when she said I had to wear this protective suit.

"All right," I said - thinking the toilet might be a "stinker", as we say in the trade.

It was an elementary error of identification. When Andy Mann appeared I thought he was Dr Manning a visiting scientist who had volunteered to help me test my newly invented shrinking ray.

PROFESSOR BUZZOFF

Dr Manning - huh! The Prof told me to stand under this machine. It didn't look much like a toilet and I was about to say that the wiring looked a bit dodgy and did she want it seeing to when she flicked a lever. Then she started getting bigger and the room started getting bigger. But hold on ... *it was me getting smaller!*

ER!

EH?

OOER!

YIKES!

ERK!

Well I know me card says no job's too small, but this job was looking, well ... a bit too small. So I went on shrinking until I got sucked into an electrical wire. "Wire am I here?" I asked meself.

There was a malfunction in the diminisher unit. By the time I managed to de-activate the ray Andy had shrunk to 0.000000025 mm, almost as small as an atom. And to make matters worse he had vanished inside the machine. Obviously this was a situation of some danger.

Yeah well, it was dangerous all right. The first thing I saw was these weird balls and I thought blimey they're atoms. And there was these tiny blips buzzing round the atoms. They were so fast they looked like a blurry mist. Well, the Prof later said they were electrons. The wire looked like this huge tunnel with atoms round the sides and there was electrons flowing through it like a river. Then I got swept away by them electrons. They was like rubbery peas and I had to swim for my life. Was I scared? Yeah, I was wetting meself. How d'you get out of this electric current Andy?

Well, me being a skilled electrician (all jobs considered by the way), I knew that an electric current is made by electrons all flowing one way. And those electrons was fast. Luckily they missed me or I would have been KILLED until I was DEAD!

Fascinating! The electrons were zapping at 1 million metres per second, and electrical signals can zip along at nearly the speed of light! Meanwhile I frantically tried to reset the shrinking ray to make Andy bigger. I switched on the light to help me see.

CLICK!

Yeah well, guess what happened? The wire got narrower. All the electrons squashed together and they slowed down and started rubbing against the atoms around the sides - yeah, and me. Phew - it was hot! Well, it's friction innit? Rubbing makes heat like when you rub your hands together.

SWEAT

ELECTRONS

ATOMS

Blobs of light started flying around - and then it hit me. *I WAS INSIDE THE LIGHT BULB.* Yeah - the one she'd just switched on. Mind you, I wasn't feeling too bright.

Of course, I didn't know that Andy was in the bulb. We scientists call the friction Andy describes "resistance" and the blobs of light Andy saw are called "photons" (fo-tonns).

PHOTON
MAGNIFIED
MILLIONS
OF TIMES

They're given off by the electrons as they try to cool down. It must have been a scientifically fascinating experience.

Yeah fascinating, Prof - shame I was about to DIE! Me protective suit was melting and I reckoned I'd be melting soon! I was boiling hot and sweating buckets. "This is it, Andy," I said to meself, "I'll never get to see the darts final!"

Just then me mobile rang. I didn't feel too chatty ... but I answered it anyway ... might as well say goodbye to someone.

RING!

I observed Andy's business card and remembered he had a mobile phone. So I called his number. I was shocked to discover that he was inside the light bulb and switched it off immediately. The switch stopped the flow of electrons and the light went out.

Just in time! The wire started to cool down - but I wasn't out of the woods yet - I mean out of the wire. I mean how was the Prof s'posed to get me out? Maybe I was going to stay tiny all me life. How was I s'posed to live? I couldn't even go outside cos an ant might tread on me and squash me flat! **ARGH!**

It took me three hours to enlarge the bulb wire in small steps and each time I cut out the portion of wire that contained Andy until eventually he was free. Then I was able to enlarge him back to his correct size. Of course, he was rather annoyed...

I'M IN THIS BIT!

A quick note

Good news! We've managed to lock Mr Sparks in the stationery cupboard so there won't be a science test – Phew!

But just in case he manages to escape here's a quick crib sheet with all the science test answers on.

Electricity Test
Answers

TOP SECRET – KEEP OUT OF REACH OF TEACHERS

MR SPARKS

1 Electrons are fast-moving blips of energy that zip around the centre of the atom.

2 The centre of the atom is called the nucleus.

3 Electrons (and the nucleus) produce electric forces.

4 An electric current is when lots of electrons are flowing together in a kind of stream.

5 Photons are blobs of light energy given out by electrons as they lose energy.

186

6 Resistance is when electrons start to rub against atoms and slow down in a wire. Resistance is also used to make heat in special wires that heat water in electric kettles and give out heat from hairdryers and electric heaters.

HAS THE KETTLE BOILED?

IT'S PUTTING UP RESISTANCE.

SHOCKING EXPRESSIONS

DO YOU KNOW ANY GOOD CONDUCTORS?

Do you say...?

WELL THERE'S MY MUSIC TEACHER. BUT SHE'S A TERRIBLE CONDUCTOR — THAT'S WHY THE SCHOOL ORCHESTRA IS SO BAD.

Answer: No, a conductor is a substance that lets electrons flow through it. Metals are good conductors because many of their outer electrons are free of their atoms and flow around anyway. And that's why electrical wires are made of copper metal.

By now you might be bursting to ask a question. Well, I don't know that for sure – you might be bursting for a pee. Anyway, your question might go like this...

Well, why not discover the next electrifying chapter and find out...?

SHOCKING DISCOVERIES

One of the most amazing things about science is the way scientists calmly tell us that tiny things exist even though no one has ever seen them.

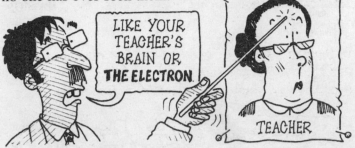

Well, lets face it they're both far too tiny to see even with the most powerful microscopes. But here's the amazing story of how it was discovered (that's the electron not your teacher's brain)...

TWO REALLY **BIG** BREAKTHROUGHS

By 1880 scientists knew how to make it and they knew how to store it (see page 215) but they didn't know what electricity was actually made of. In that year scientist William Crookes built a new machine to help him find the answer...

CATHODE RAY TUBE

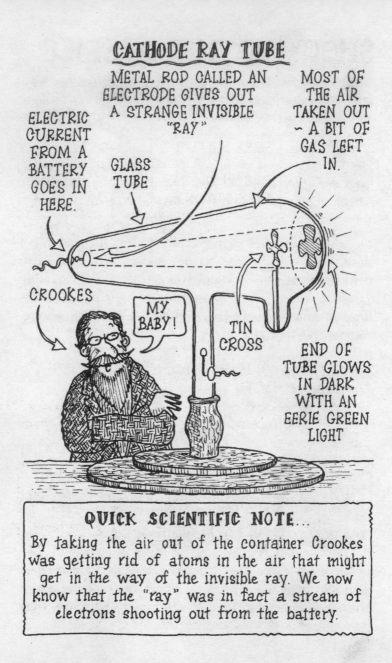

METAL ROD CALLED AN ELECTRODE GIVES OUT A STRANGE INVISIBLE "RAY"

MOST OF THE AIR TAKEN OUT ~ A BIT OF GAS LEFT IN.

ELECTRIC CURRENT FROM A BATTERY GOES IN HERE.

GLASS TUBE

CROOKES

MY BABY!

TIN CROSS

END OF TUBE GLOWS IN DARK WITH AN EERIE GREEN LIGHT

QUICK SCIENTIFIC NOTE...

By taking the air out of the container Crookes was getting rid of atoms in the air that might get in the way of the invisible ray. We now know that the "ray" was in fact a stream of electrons shooting out from the battery.

COULD YOU BE A SCIENTIST?

So what do you think made the green glow?
a) The gas glowing as it's hit by the electrons.
b) The glass tube glowing where the electrons hit it.
c) A chemical reaction between the gas and the chemicals in the glass.

> **Answer: b)** The electrons hit the atoms of the glass and heated them up until they gave out energy in the form of light photons.

Of course, Crookes didn't know all this and he didn't understand what he was seeing. And as you're about to discover it was hard for Crookes to explain his work to other scientists because they didn't trust him. The problem was that, unlike most scientists, Crookes believed in *ghosts*. Here's his story...

Hall of fame: William Crookes (1832–1919)
Nationality: British
Crookes was the oldest of 16 kids. (Would you like 15 cheeky little brothers and sisters breaking your things?)

Obviously this could drive a person to desperate measures and maybe that's why Crookes became a chemistry teacher. But eventually he inherited a fortune. (So at least he could afford Christmas presents for everyone.)

He retired from teaching and set up his own private chemistry lab for exciting experiments.

But some of his investigations shocked other scientists. In those days many people believed that the spirits of the dead came back as ghosts and could be summoned by people with special abilities called mediums. Crookes decided to find the truth by careful scientific observation...

THE SECRET DIARY OF WILLIAM CROOKES

~ 11 November 1870 ~

Tonight I set up an experiment with medium Florence Cook. I had heard of her reputation for making ghosts appear but nothing was to prepare me for what I saw. We sat in a dark room and the medium went into a trance. Her eyes closed and she started breathing quickly and deeply. "Is there anyone there?" she called out.

RAP!

There was a sudden rap on the table.

F.C.

"Rap once for yes," demanded the medium.
Bang!
"Are you a spirit?"
Another rap.
"Can you make yourself visible?"
I asked, sounding rather scared.
A cold wind blew through the room. The curtain fluttered and I saw a vague white shape. I blinked in horror - it was a woman with a ghostly pale face. She drifted round the room and I almost managed to touch her unearthly form.
"Who ... what are you?" I gasped. The ghost moved her pale lips. In a faint voice she replied: "My name is Katie, I have a message for you..."
The medium gave a sudden cry. She was pale and sweaty now, and when I looked again the ghost had vanished. So what was the message? I can't wait for the next session!

But had he seen a real ghost? Crookes' fellow scientists were less than impressed with his work as a spectre inspector. Most scientists don't believe in ghosts (I suppose they can see right through them) and they thought that Crookes didn't stand a ghost of a chance of proving anything. Instead the investigation ruined Crookes' image as a sensible scientist.

One scientist who didn't give up on Crookes was John Joseph Thomson (1856–1940), a professor at Cambridge University. JJ, as his friends called him, was useless at experiments and usually broke his equipment (but blowing up the school lab is not always a sign of genius as I'm sure your teacher will point out). Luckily for JJ, when he became a professor he had people to do the hands-on work for him.

WHERE'S JENKINS?

STILL IN HOSPITAL, SIR. YOU BLEW HIM UP LAST WEEK.

JJ thought the "ray" Crookes had reported might be made of tiny blips of energy and to find out more he repeated one of Crookes' tests of using a magnet to bend the ray. He worked out how strong the magnetic force had to be to bend the ray and using complicated maths he calculated the weight of the blips that he thought made up the ray from the angle it was bent. Try doing that for your maths homework!

CAN I HAVE SOME ART HOMEWORK INSTEAD?

It turned out the ray really *was* made of tiny blips and they were far lighter than the lightest atoms. Thomson calculated how much energy each blip carried and realized that it matched the lightest atoms. Thomson reckoned rightly that each atom carried at least one and usually far more of the blips. The tiny blips, of course, were electrons.

Bet you never knew!
Electrons make things feel solid. You see, the electrical force made by an electron pushes other electrons away. Solid objects are made of atoms and electrons tightly packed together and so when you squash them they push apart slightly and this makes the object feel solid. Just think – if it wasn't for electrons, sitting on a chair would be like sitting on a slimy school dinner blancmange. You'd sink through it and end up sprawled on your bum.

ELECTRONS – WHO NEEDS 'EM?

SPLOSH!

Electric forces can do lots of other interesting things. They can even make your hair stand on end! And you can find out how in the next chapter – it's bound to set a few sparks flying.

I'D BETTER READ ON...

SHOCKING STATIC ELECTRICITY

Have you ever got an electric shock when stroking the cat or trying on a woolly jumper? Yes? CONGRATULATIONS – you've encountered static electricity. But "static" is definitely the wrong word. After all "static" means staying still...

So you'd think that in static electricity the electrons must be lazing around reading comics. WRONG! Actually, although the electrons aren't all flowing together in an electric current, they're still whizzing around as usual. And in static electricity the electrons also get to fly through the air and make sparks and give scientists nasty shocks and many other exciting things.

Wanna know more?

Before you can understand the secret of static you need to get your brain-box round the electrical forces made by an electron and the atom nucleus. This quickie experiment should help...

Dare you discover ... how electric forces work?

You will need:
Two magnets

What you do:
Put them close together.

What happens...?

a) The magnets spring apart or pull together depending on which way round they are.

b) The magnets are *always* drawn together.

c) The magnets can be placed together but you don't feel any force between them.

> **Answer: a)** When the magnets spring apart you can imagine that they are two electrons. As you may recall from page 195 the electrons are pushed apart by their own forces.

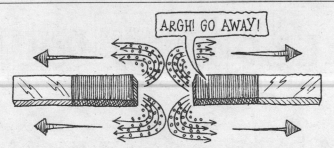

When the magnets pull together you can imagine they're like an electron and a nucleus. This time their forces actually pull them together! (It's all to do with complex interactions between the two forces and no, I don't understand this either.)

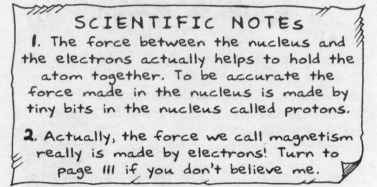

SCIENTIFIC NOTES

1. The force between the nucleus and the electrons actually helps to hold the atom together. To be accurate the force made in the nucleus is made by tiny bits in the nucleus called protons.

2. Actually, the force we call magnetism really is made by electrons! Turn to page 111 if you don't believe me.

SHOCKING EXPRESSIONS

Two scientists are talking...

Are they comparing hotel bills?

Answer: No, they're talking about their experiments. To avoid confusion, scientists call all the electrical energy carried by the electron a NEGATIVE charge and the electrical energy carried by the nucleus a POSITIVE charge. And you'll be positively thrilled to know these terms will be coming up a lot in the next few pages.

Now here's another glimpse of our pals the Atom family as they show you how they make static electricity...

WE'LL NEED A BALLOON AND A CAT.

1 We rub the balloon on the cat's fur ten times or more.

199

2 The Atom family are living on the cat's fluff.

The atoms of the balloon are rubbing electrons free from the atoms of the cat fluff. Here's a close-up view of what happens to them...

3 The electrons are now stranded on the balloon's surface. Of course this means there's a lot of electron energy (negative charge, remember?) on the balloon.

4 The powerful negative charge made by the electrons results in a negative force that tries to pull on the atoms of the cat's fluff.

5 Meanwhile on the cat's fluff, the atoms that are missing their electrons are positively charged. And together their positive electrical forces try to pull the electrons back.

6 These forces make the cat's fur stand up on end as they try to pull the balloon and cat together.

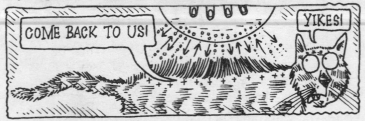

7 When the balloon is brought nearer to the cat's fur the missing electrons are yanked back to their atoms. You can even hear this happen as a quiet crackle.

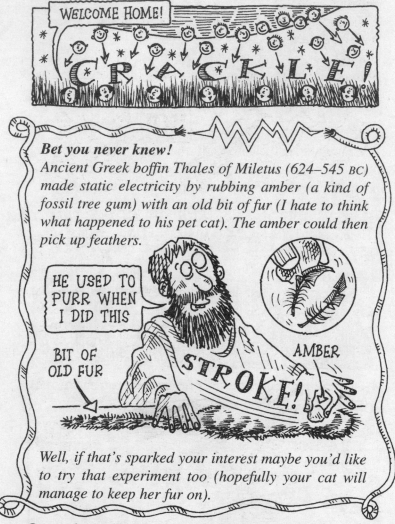

WELCOME HOME!

C·R·A·C·K·L·E!

Bet you never knew!
Ancient Greek boffin Thales of Miletus (624–545 BC) made static electricity by rubbing amber (a kind of fossil tree gum) with an old bit of fur (I hate to think what happened to his pet cat). The amber could then pick up feathers.

HE USED TO PURR WHEN I DID THIS

BIT OF OLD FUR

STROKE!

AMBER

Well, if that's sparked your interest maybe you'd like to try that experiment too (hopefully your cat will manage to keep her fur on).

Or maybe you'd like to try this experiment...

Dare you discover ... how to make clingfilm move?

You will need:

Two pieces of new clingfilm 10 cm x 2 cm

A clean dry comb

Blutak

Some clean hair – you might possibly find some on your head. (If not maybe you could ask the cat nicely.)

What you do:

1 Hold a piece of clingfilm in each hand. Try to bring the two pieces of clingfilm together. Notice what happens.

2 Stick a piece of clingfilm to the end of a table so the clingfilm hangs downwards. Now comb your hair quickly and strongly four times. Quickly point the teeth of the comb towards the strip of clingfilm and hold it close but not touching. Notice what happens.

Well, what does happen?

a) The two pieces of clingfilm are drawn together. But the clingfilm doesn't want to touch the comb.

b) The pieces of clingfilm don't want to touch but the clingfilm does want to touch the comb.

c) A spark flies between the clingfilm and comb but nothing happens between the two bits of clingfilm.

Answer: b) The atoms of the clingfilm are short of electrons. This means they are positively charged and give out positive forces. Remember how two negative forces push each other away? Well, two positive forces also push against each other and that's why the pieces of clingfilm move apart. The comb rips electrons off your hairs and the force from these electrons (negative charge) pulls in the positively charged atoms in the clingfilm.

SUPER STATIC

Static electricity is shockingly useful. For example, did you know that photocopiers use static electricity to copy documents?

Here's what happens...

1 A bright light shines on the picture to be copied and its image reflects on to a mirror and through a lens on to a metal drum. Got all that?

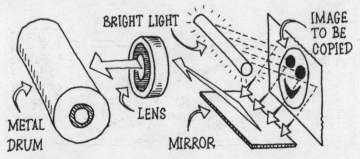

2 The drum is coated with a substance called selenium (see-leen-nee-um) that gives off electrons when light shines on it.

3 This means the areas of the drum that get most light (in other words the brighter parts of the original) lose negatively charged electrons and become positively charged. Yep – it pays to think positive!

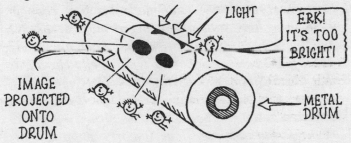

4 Positively charged toner powder gets sprinkled on the drum and sticks to the dark areas which are still negatively charged. (Hope you're taking notes on all this.)

5 Paper now goes over the drum and the toner sticks to the paper to make a copy of the original picture.

6 A heater softens the toner and squashes it on to the paper.

7 *Finito* – one perfect photocopy!

Bet you never knew!

The photocopier was invented by US inventor Chester Carlson (1906–1968) who made his first copy in 1938 using tiny statically charged moss seeds. He must have been ex-static – ha ha. After all, it had taken four years of tinkering with smelly chemicals that filled Chester's flat with rotten farty egg whiffs. On the way his marriage broke up, his research assistant resigned, and countless firms refused to back him. But after more than 20 years of improvements photocopiers became popular and Chester became a multi-millionaire.

But Chester's discovery wouldn't have been possible without the work of earlier scientists who investigated static electricity. Did you know some of the most shocking static electricity experiments were performed by a scientist called Stephen Gray (1666–1736)? And can you believe he conducted these experiments on ... helpless children. Now read on for the whole shocking story...

A SHOCKING STORY

London 1730

"You new here?" asked Joe.

The thin little girl with the dirty face nodded dumbly.

"And that's why you were following me about just now?"

The girl nodded again.

Joe chewed his lip as he pondered what to do. He didn't want some little kid following him around all day but he could see the new girl was scared of being in the children's home.

They sat down cross-legged on the bare dusty floor and he asked her name.

"Hannah." the girl whispered as if scared to raise her voice.

"Well Hannah, it's not so bad in here. Look, I tell you what, here's a story to take your mind off it."

The girl leaned forward expectantly.

"Is it a true story?"

"It's true all right," said Joe. "I was working for this scientist and guess what – he did experiments on me!"

"You mean it – actual science experiments?" asked the girl.

"Stop asking questions and I'll tell you. It happened one day when this old scientist geezer came to the children's home and asked for a kid to help him with his work. He was fat and rich and his name was Mr Gray, Mr Stephen Gray.

"Well, the supervisor collared me and took me to Mr Gray's place. Real posh it was with heavy curtains and a smell of polish and silver on the table. And guess what? Mr Gray gave me a slap-up meal! Said I looked as if I could do with feeding! I had beef and onions and dumplings and potatoes and gravy and three helpings of pudding. Heaven it was."

Joe glanced at Hannah and sure enough she was drooling. "I want to work for Mr Gray too!" she said hungrily.

"Mr Gray's servant came in. She was this really old grim-looking woman named Mrs Salter, and she said 'If the boy eats any more he will break his cords.' *Cords*? I thought. Well, that made me a bit scared. Maybe this Gray bloke was going to tie me up and then he was going to *kill* me. *Maybe he was going to chop my body up and eat me!*

"Mr Gray must have seen my expression because he patted me on the head and said 'Don't worry Joseph, it won't hurt much.'"

"Did it hurt?" asked Hannah fearfully.

"Well," said Joe bravely, "I'm still alive, ain't I? Anyway, Mr Gray took me into this room and I was gobsmacked. It was stacked with all these scientific gadgets, like glass rods, a set of metal balls – I didn't know what they was for – and flasks and telescopes.

"Mr Gray picked up a telescope. 'I used to be an astronomer till I did my back in bending over that telescope. Well, now I'm into electricity.'

"'What's electricity?' I asked, and Mr Gray told me all about this weird force. Well, don't ask me to explain it. I couldn't get me head round it.

"'Is that anything to do with them metal balls?' I mumbled stupidly.

"'Ah yes – interesting they are,' said Mr Gray. 'I proved that it doesn't matter if a ball is hollow or solid – it can still store the same amount of static electricity. I think the force must be stored on the outside of the ball. And I learnt how to electrify objects and that brings us to our experiment.'

"He nodded to Mrs Salter and quick as a flash she looped silk cords round my shoulders and legs and waist. I was too surprised to say anything. But I yelled loud enough when they hoisted me into the air. I thought me dinner was going to come up all over the floor.

"Mr Gray put his finger on his lips. 'Don't shout, Joseph. We're only going to electrify you.'

"'But I don't want to be electrified!' I yelled.

"Mr Gray looked troubled. 'But it's for science, Joseph and anyway, I'll pay you sixpence.'

"Well, that settled it. I'd have done it for a penny.

"I felt really weird like I was swimming – or maybe flying in the air with my arms outstretched on either side. Mrs Salter rubbed my clothes real hard with a glass rod

– blimey was she strong! Meanwhile Mr Gray put some tiny bits of paper on three metal plates on the ground under me.

"'Now, Joseph,' said Mr Gray, 'reach out your hands and pick up those bits of paper.'

"'I can't do that!' I cried. My arms were too short to reach the paper and just to show him I tried. And something magic happened. The bits of paper flew towards my fingers – they looked just like confetti at a wedding.

"'Bravo!' shouted Mr Gray clapping his big fat hands and I was so chuffed I gave him a mid-air bow.

"'Can I come down now?' I asked. Mr Gray nodded and his servant reached out to untie me. There was a sudden crack and I felt a sharp pain. It was agony!

"'Oh dear,' said Mr Gray, 'you seem to have received an electric shock. Never mind here's your sixpence.'"

"You really got a whole sixpence?" asked Hannah, her eyes widening.

"Yes," said Joseph proudly.

"That's a lot of money. I've never seen one. Can I see it? Can I touch it?"

Joe held the shining silver coin and the girl touched his hand.

"Ow!" she yelled. "You stung me!"

"Don't worry," said the boy with a careless wave of his hand. "It's just an electric shock."

Dare you discover ... how Joe picked up the paper?

You will need:

A piece of polystyrene (to represent Joe)
A woollen jumper or pair of nylon tights
A few tiny bits of paper (the circles of paper from a hole punch are ideal)

What you do:

1 Rub the polystyrene on the fabric a few times.
2 Hold the polystyrene near the bits of paper.

What happens?

a) The bits of paper jump on to the polystyrene.
b) You get an electric shock.
c) The polystyrene is pulled gently towards the paper.

Answer: a) When Joe was rubbed with the rod, the glass removed electrons from his clothes and skin. This gave the atoms that made them up a positive charge. The electrons in the paper were pulled towards him and this pulled the paper too. When Mrs Salter touched Joe electrons from her skin also rushed on to Joe and gave him a shock.

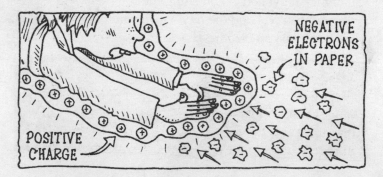

Oh, by the way, Hannah didn't get a shock because Joe was still electrified – it's just that skin sometimes collects an electric charge (for example when you walk over a carpet). That's why you can get a shock by touching people.

IT'S SUCH A SHOCK TO MEET YOU!

Bet you never knew!
Besides electrifying a boy, Gray found he could electrify hair and feathers. It's even said that he sent electricity along gold-painted cow guts. (Don't ask me what he was doing painting cow guts gold!)

SIXPENCE? I'LL WANT A LOT MORE THAN THAT, PAL!

He investigated different conductors (and if you don't know what they are check back to page 188 at once!).

SO WHAT HAPPENED NEXT?
In 1732 brave French scientist Charles Dufay (1698–1739) repeated Gray's experiment using himself instead

of a boy. According to one story, when Dufay's assistant tried to touch him, the scientist got a shock that burnt through his waistcoat.

The scientist found the experience thrilling – or should I say electrifying (ha ha) – and insisted on repeating it in the dark so that he could see the spark made by the static electricity.

Dufay's experiments proved that anything could be electrically charged by rubbing except for liquids, metals and a grisly lump of meat. Dufay didn't realize this, but since these substances are good conductors of electricity, electrons tend to run through them rather than sticking around to build up a powerful negative electric charge.

Within a few years scientists developed brilliant machines that could make and store static electricity if it was needed for experiments. (In those days mains electricity hadn't been invented.) Would you fancy owning one of these machines? Of course you wouldn't use it to give nasty shocks to your teacher/brother/sister would you? WOULD YOU?

A SHOCKING CATALOGUE

Amaze your friends and shock your enemies with this incredible range of static electricity generators from SPARKY-JOLT LTD.

You'll love a Leyden Jar!

Developed by Dutch scientist Pieter van Musschenbroek (1692-1761) this stylish jar stores static electricity.

METAL BALL

METAL CHAIN

WATER IN GLASS JAR

STATIC ELECTRICITY PASSES DOWN METAL CHAIN INTO JAR AND CAN'T ESCAPE.

X-RAY VIEW OF GLASS JAR WITH METAL LINING BOTH INSIDE AND OUT

SHOCKING SAFETY WARNING!

Touch the metal ball at the top and you'll get a painful electric shock. This shocking discovery was made accidentally by Musschenbroek's assistant. Ouch!

D'YOU MEAN THIS BIT?... ARGH!

You'll wonder at a Wimshurst!

Named after its inventor James Wimshurst (1832–1903), this wonderful piece of electric wizardry makes static electricity when the glass and metal discs rub together.

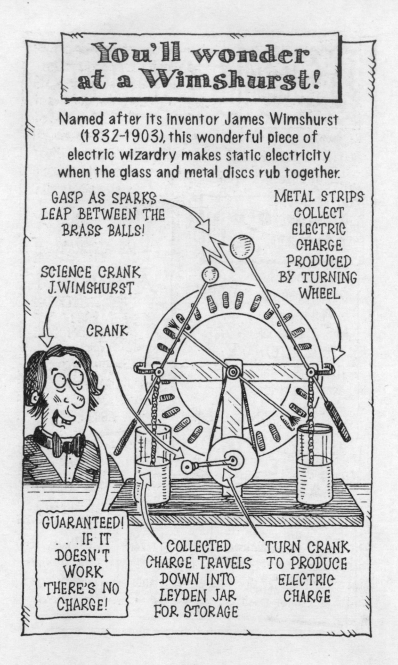

GASP AS SPARKS LEAP BETWEEN THE BRASS BALLS!

METAL STRIPS COLLECT ELECTRIC CHARGE PRODUCED BY TURNING WHEEL

SCIENCE CRANK J.WIMSHURST

CRANK

GUARANTEED! ...IF IT DOESN'T WORK THERE'S NO CHARGE!

COLLECTED CHARGE TRAVELS DOWN INTO LEYDEN JAR FOR STORAGE

TURN CRANK TO PRODUCE ELECTRIC CHARGE

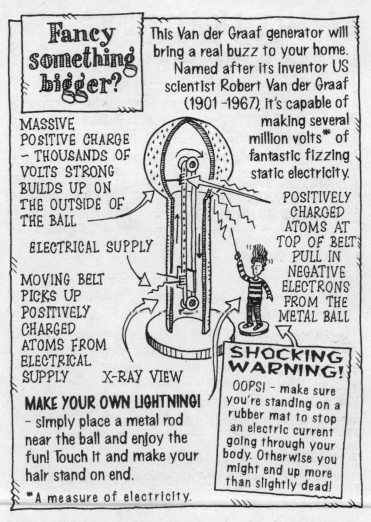

Fancy something bigger?

This Van der Graaf generator will bring a real buzz to your home. Named after its inventor US scientist Robert Van der Graaf (1901-1967), it's capable of making several million volts* of fantastic fizzing static electricity.

MASSIVE POSITIVE CHARGE - THOUSANDS OF VOLTS STRONG BUILDS UP ON THE OUTSIDE OF THE BALL

POSITIVELY CHARGED ATOMS AT TOP OF BELT PULL IN NEGATIVE ELECTRONS FROM THE METAL BALL

ELECTRICAL SUPPLY

MOVING BELT PICKS UP POSITIVELY CHARGED ATOMS FROM ELECTRICAL SUPPLY

X-RAY VIEW

MAKE YOUR OWN LIGHTNING!
- simply place a metal rod near the ball and enjoy the fun! Touch it and make your hair stand on end.

*A measure of electricity.

SHOCKING WARNING!
OOPS! - make sure you're standing on a rubber mat to stop an electric current going through your body. Otherwise you might end up more than slightly dead!

Did anyone mention lightning? Well, you may be thunderstruck to discover that lightning is a form of static electricity. And if that came like a bolt from the blue you really ought to read the next chapter. You're bound to find it striking!

LETHAL LIGHTNING

TEACHER'S TEA-BREAK TEASER

Try this shockingly tricky question on your teacher...

HOW CAN WATER START A FIRE?

STAFF

Clue: it's to do with static electricity.

Answer: Sometimes when oil tanker holds are being cleaned with high pressure hoses, atoms in the water rub together really fast. This makes static electricity that results in lightning sparks. The sparks can set fire to petrol fumes in the hold and blow up the tanker!

But how do water drops make lightning? If you're a bright spark you'll read on and find out!

Shocking electricity fact file

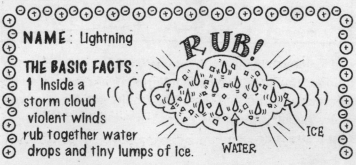

NAME: Lightning

THE BASIC FACTS:
1 Inside a storm cloud violent winds rub together water drops and tiny lumps of ice.

RUB!

WATER   ICE

SWOOP!

2 The ice loses electrons to the water and gets swept upwards.

NEGATIVELY CHARGED WATER

3 The drops of water tend to fall downwards (yes – they're called rain) so the top of the cloud without electrons becomes positively charged and the bottom, with all those electrons, is negatively charged.

POSITIVE

NEGATIVE

YIKES!

RUMBLE!

+ + + + + + + +

4 The powerful negative charge in the base of the cloud makes a force that pushes away negatively charged electrons on the ground. This leaves an area of positively charged atoms.

219

THE SHOCKING DETAILS:

1 A bolt of lightning strikes at 1,600 km a second.

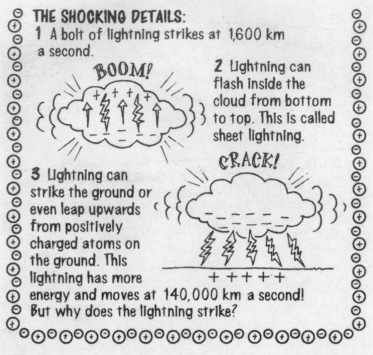

2 Lightning can flash inside the cloud from bottom to top. This is called sheet lightning.

3 Lightning can strike the ground or even leap upwards from positively charged atoms on the ground. This lightning has more energy and moves at 140,000 km a second! But why does the lightning strike?

Obviously anyone who tries to find out is taking a very big risk – a VERY BIG RISK.

A FLASHY JOB

Professor Buzzoff wanted to film lightning in ultra-slow motion. But who could she ask to take on this ultra-dangerous job? There was only one person in the frame.

I assured Andy that no shrinking was required and that I would join him on the shoot. After a brief discussion about money he agreed to take the job.

I took the job cos I'm a dab hand with camcorders. I do weddings, funerals, whatever (all offers considered). So filming lightning seemed a cinch - I mean, it's all over in a flash, innit? So there I was filming the clouds and waiting for a flash of lightning and I cricked me neck looking up and got a right soaking. "Water rotten job!" I said to meself...

Andy didn't have too long to wait. When the negative charge at the bottom of the cloud reaches a certain power, the lightning appears as a bright blob under the cloud. This is actually a ball of negatively charged electrons.

A stream of electrons flashes downwards, drawn by the pulling force of the positively charged atoms on the ground. What we call the streak of lightning marks the path taken by the electrons through the atoms of the air. On the way, the lightning hits atoms in the air making them give off heat and light. The lightning appears much brighter.

The lightning hits the ground. The bolt of lightning is up to 1 cm wide.

The lightning heats up the air around it very quickly, then it cools again very quickly. This creates shock waves in the air that our ears hear as thunder. As Andy was taking this picture I became aware that another bolt of lightning was forming in the cloud under which he was standing...

Did someone say "All over in a flash"? Didn't realize it would be over for _me_ in a flash. I was too busy filming the Prof (who was jumping up and down pointing to something high above me) to see the next streak coming. Fast as lightning it was.... Argh!

THIS IS A NEWS FLASH. ANDY MANN HAS BEEN STRUCK BY LIGHTNING! WE'LL BE HEADING OVER TO THE HOSPITAL IN A FEW MINUTES TO CHECK ON HIS CONDITION.

So YOU'RE not scared of lightning? And you fancy making some lightning in the comfort of your own home? OK – here's how; but try not to fire your lightning at little brothers or sisters or the cat – Tiddles has suffered enough!

Dare you discover ... how to make lightning?

You will need:

A radio with the aerial extended

A balloon

A thick jumper (no not a stupid kangaroo – I mean a *woollen* jumper). A woollen rug or scarf will also do.

What you do:

1 Wait until it gets dark or sit in the coal cellar with the lights out. This experiment works best in complete darkness.

2 Rub the balloon on the wool about ten times. Put it near or touching the aerial.

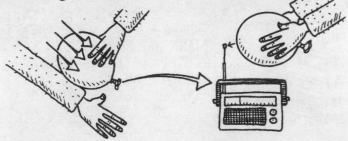

What do you see?

a) The radio comes on without you touching it – it's spooky.

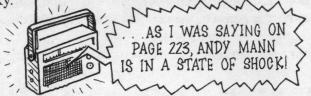

...AS I WAS SAYING ON PAGE 223, ANDY MANN IS IN A STATE OF SHOCK!

b) An eerie glowing ball of light appears and floats round the room – scaring the life out of your pet budgie.

c) Tiny sparks.

Dare you discover ... how to hear lightning?

You will need:

The same equipment from the first experiment

What you do:

1 Switch the radio to AM and make sure it's not tuned to any station.

2 Turn the volume down very low.

3 Repeat the first experiment and listen.

HMMM!

What do you hear?

a) Pop music even though the radio isn't tuned.

b) A quiet pop (but it isn't music).

c) You hear the sound in **b)** but it's REALLY LOUD.

Answers:

1 c) These are electrons stripped off the wool jumping from the balloon to the radio aerial. The sparks are basically tiny flashes of lightning.

2 b) You are listening to electrons jumping from the balloon to the radio aerial. If you switch on the radio during a thunderstorm tuned as before you will hear the same noise but this time it will be made by lightning. Mind you, you won't have been the first to investigate this sizzling force of nature.

Hall of fame: Benjamin Franklin (1706–1790)
Nationality: American

Benjamin Franklin packed so much into his life it's a wonder that he had time to eat or sleep. He was a...

Young Ben was the youngest of 17 children – can you imagine how terrible that must have been? Sixteen older brothers and sisters bossing you around and getting their baths first so you have to make do with their filthy scummy bath water? Ben had just three years of schooling but that must have seemed too long because he hated maths and failed all his tests. But worse was to follow – he had to spend the next seven years working 12 hours a day for no pay for one of his older brothers. Would you swap school for this?

Ben learnt the art of printing in his brother's shop. Then suddenly at the ripe old age of 15, he found himself a *newspaper editor.*

Ben's brother had been locked up for saying rude things about important people in the newspaper he printed. So Ben took charge of the newspaper and that must have been really cool. He could have printed wicked articles about computer games and rollerblading. If they'd been invented then, that is.

Ben eventually fell out with his brother and went to Philadelphia, arriving with just a small loaf of bread to eat and no money at all. Luckily, he soon found work as a printer and became pals with the British Governor who ruled the city in those days. But the Governor played a shocking trick on young Ben. He sent him to London to learn more about printing but after Ben set sail he realized that the Governor hadn't given him the money he'd promised.

Ben's big break came in 1732. He was back in Pennsylvania after a spell as a printer in London and he published an almanac – a sort of calendar with wise sayings. It was an instant smash-hit! The sayings are so well-known and wise you might have heard your granny use them...

Actually, Ben Franklin *didn't* take his own advice. When he lived in Paris in the 1770s he enjoyed lots of late-night parties, but he still remained healthy and rich, and as you're about to find out he was wise too. Mention this to your granny ... *if you dare!*

Ben made so much money he retired from printing and got interested in science and inventing things. Amongst other things he invented a new kind of wood-burning stove, extendable grippers for taking things off high shelves (and raiding the biscuit jar) and a musical instrument made of a glass bowl with a wet rim. The glass bowl turned round and if you touched the rim with your fingertips it made a sound.

Bet you never knew!
Benjamin Franklin was interested in everything – including farting. He set up a competition to discover a drug that could be mixed with food to make pleasant perfumed farts. Although such a discovery is not to be sniffed at, sadly there were no winners.

But Ben's greatest discoveries were to do with electricity. In 1746 he went to a science talk on electricity and he was so thrilled by it that he bought up all the lecturer's equipment and started doing his own experiments.

Bet you never knew!
Franklin was a great scientist and he wasn't afraid to suggest new ideas. He was the first to suggest that static electricity might be based on positive and negative charges. (He didn't have too much proof of that but he was right of course.) Unfortunately Ben reckoned that electricity flowed from positive areas to negative areas. He was wrong – negatively charged electrons flow towards the positively charged atoms.

Like other experimenters, Franklin made sparks from electrically charged Leyden jars and the sight of the spark and the tiny crack it made reminded him of lightning. Could lightning be a giant electrical spark? Ben wondered. And if so, how could he prove it?

His first plan was to put a metal rod on top of a church steeple and draw off some of the electric charge from a thunder cloud. But the church steeple he had in mind hadn't been built and within a few months a French scientist followed Ben's plan and performed the test. It proved that lightning was indeed made of electricity – but it was really dangerous. If lightning hit the metal pole anyone close by would meet a shocking end. As Russian scientists Georg Richmann found out to his cost...

The St. Petersburg Times

RUSSIAN RICHMANN ROASTED!

by ace reporter Hall D. Frontpage

Top scientist Georg Richmann has been struck dead by lightning. The Russian boffin was seen rushing home to perform a dangerous experiment. Richmann, 42, wanted to measure the strength of the electric charge of a bolt of lightning. Today the Times talks to his long-time friend Mikhail Lomonosov.

"I tried to warn him. I said 'Georg, Franklin says electricity can jump from the lightning rod.' But did he listen? Silly idiot only put a metal ruler up close to the rod. He had a thread on the ruler and he wanted to measure how far the charge would lift the thread up.

"Yeah - it was a shocking error!

A giant spark shot out of the rod. It bounced off the ruler and struck Georg dead. I was thunderstruck! So was Georg and well, when I saw what the bolt had done to Georg, I bolted too. A pretty sight it was not."

Scorched shape in carpet shocks servants

By that time, Benjamin Franklin had conducted his own experiment on lightning. Of course, it was extremely dangerous, as you've just discovered. So did Ben share Richmann's fate and end up a fried Franklin-furter?

BENJAMIN FRANKLIN'S NOTEBOOK

1 October 1752

HANDKERCHIEF (BIT OF DRIED SNOT)

STRING WITH KEY ON THE END

METAL SPIKE TIED TO KITE

SILK THREAD (SILK CAN'T CARRY AN ELECTRICAL CHARGE)

Dark overcast day, really thundery, looks like rain. Great! It's ideal weather for my kite flying test. I've made a special kite from an old silk handkerchief.

My plan is to fly the kite in a thunderstorm and pick up some electricity from the clouds, which will run down the string and charge up the key. But will it work? It's not the danger of getting killed that bothers me - it's getting killed in public. I think I'd die of embarrassment. So it's just me and my son and we're going to a nice quiet field where no one can see us.

Three hours later. . .

This is really frustrating. There's no decent thunderclouds blowing our way - my lad's really bored. Oh well, better give up. No - hold on, here comes one.

Now to get this kite in the air! Wow! The threads on the string are standing on end - I figure they're electrified. I'm electrified too - with excitement. Let's put my hand near that key - better not touch it - OUCH!!! I got a painful electric shock. I'm so happy YES! YES! YES! Let's put a Leyden jar up to the key. There's a spark jumping into the jar - it's the static electricity I've been studying. Well that proves it. I've managed to draw electricity from the clouds and I'm still alive!

HORRIBLE HEALTH WARNING!

Franklin and his son were dead lucky - but they could have been unlucky and dead. If the kite had been struck by lightning then Ben would have been a has-Ben sorry, a has-been. Don't ever, EVER fly a kite in a thunderstorm or near high-voltage power lines.

Following this success Ben was soon hard at work designing an invention that would prevent lightning from striking your house and giving the cat a nervous breakdown.

IS YOUR HOUSE SAFE?

LIGHTNING CAN STRIKE ANYWHERE, SO WHY NOT FIT ONE OF BEN FRANKLIN'S NEW-FANGLED LIGHTNING CONDUCTORS?

Negative charge in thunderclouds forces electrons from the tip of the rod. This means the atoms there are positively charged.

Negatively charged lightning drawn to the rod and runs down wire and safely into the ground.

DELUXE VERSION
As used by Ben Franklin in his own home. For a modest extra cost you can have the wire running inside your home so you can do science experiments each time the rod gets struck by lightning. It comes complete with real brass bells that ring when the electrical current makes them move.

DELUXE VERSION SHOWN ON THIS SIDE OF THE HOUSE

DING-A-LING!

WELL STRIKE ME DOWN!

Ben's discoveries made him famous. In those days North America was ruled by Britain but in 1776 Ben helped write the American Declaration of Independence. (It's said his co-authors had to keep an eye on Ben to stop him putting in silly jokes.) Ben became America's ambassador in France and won French support for the new nation.

Now back to lightning...

Bet you never knew!

In Victorian times some people carried lightning conductors on the end of their umbrellas. The device consisted of a metal rod on the spike of the umbrella, with a metal wire attached down which the lightning would run (and hopefully away from the petrified person holding the brolly). It worked in the same way as a full-sized conductor and was designed to keep its owner safe in a storm. But was this a smart idea? I mean, these umbrellas attracted lightning – would you put up with one?

WARNING! PURCHASERS WERE ADVISED NOT TO USE THE METAL WIRE TO WALK THE DOG

TEACHER'S TEA-BREAK TEASER

Are you fond of boiled fish? Well, if not you might have some left over from your school dinner. Hammer boldly on the staffroom door. When it squeaks open, smile sweetly, and shove the revolting fish dish under your teacher's nose saying...

Answer: It depends on how close the fish was. As you know, electricity can travel though water. Any fish close to the strike would get a massive electric shock and the heat from the strike would probably boil it too. The heat turns the water to steam and makes an explosion that can be heard underwater for many kilometres. Any divers close by would probably be deafened.

LIGHTNING ADDITION QUIZ

This quiz is really easy. In fact, you can probably go through it like greased lightning, ha ha. All you have to do is to add up the numbers.

1 How many times does lightning strike somewhere in the world in a second? The answer = 14 + 86

2 What is the record number of times a person has been struck by lightning? The answer = answer **1** – 93

3 Lightning is hotter than the surface of the sun. By how many times? The answer = answer **2** – 1.5

4 In 1995 lightning struck a football match. How many were blasted by a single bolt? The answer = answer **3** + 11.5

Answers:

1 100. Luckily it isn't the same spot – after all, lightning never strikes twice in the same place, so they say. Mind you, some people do seem to get more than their fair share of lightning strikes...

2 7. US park ranger Roy Sullivan was struck *seven* times. That's at seven *different* times – not all on the same day. That really would have put him off his tea. In 1942 he lost his toenail (he must have been cut to the quick); in 1969 his eyebrows were burnt off; the following year his shoulder was burnt; in 1972 and 1973 his hair caught fire – "hair we go again", as he might have said; in 1976 his ankle was injured; and in 1977 his chest was burnt ... but I expect he was getting used to it by then.

3 5.5. Lightning can be 30,000°C (54,000°F) and the surface of the sun is a rather tepid 5,530°C (9,980°F). No wonder a lightning strike can melt solid rock – and that's not your auntie's rock cakes we're talking about here. (They'd probably survive intact.)

4 17. The victims were all parents and children from Kent, England. They all survived, but some of them suffered nasty burns.

Now, how about poor old Andy Mann – is he badly burned too? Is he *still alive*? Let's grab a bunch of grapes and rush over to the hospital.

A CHECK ON ANDY MANN

The good news is that Andy is sitting up in his hospital bed and watching the darts final on TV. The bad news is that he's suffered a few injuries.

PATIENT RECORD

STRICTLY CONFIDENTIAL

NAME: Andy Mann   **Age:** 35

GENERAL NOTE: This patient has a severe attitude problem. He has been complaining loudly about a Professor Buzzoff.

SYMPTOMS: The patient shows signs of having been struck by lightning.

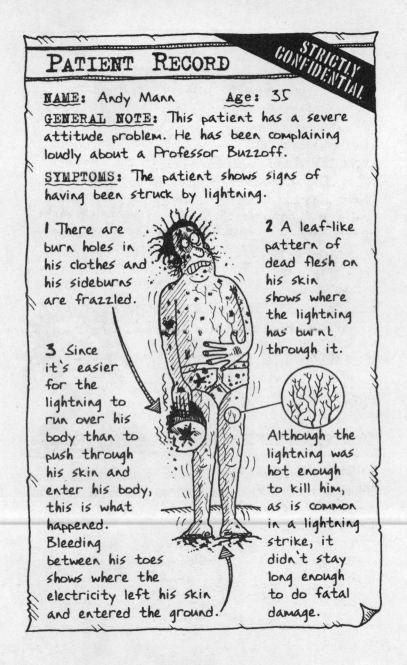

1 There are burn holes in his clothes and his sideburns are frazzled.

2 A leaf-like pattern of dead flesh on his skin shows where the lightning has burnt through it.

3 Since it's easier for the lightning to run over his body than to push through his skin and enter his body, this is what happened. Bleeding between his toes shows where the electricity left his skin and entered the ground.

Although the lightning was hot enough to kill him, as is common in a lightning strike, it didn't stay long enough to do fatal damage.

FORCED AIR

CLONK!

4 The patient was knocked out for about a minute. This was caused by the force of air pushed ahead of the lightning bolt. He was lucky not to suffer broken bones.

<u>PROGNOSIS</u>: If the lightning had actually gone through the patient's body the shock of being struck by lightning might have made his heart stop and resulted in death. As it is – he's lucky to be alive but should make a full recovery.

HUH ~ ME LUCKY? ME BOILERSUIT'S RUINED, ME EARRING'S MELTED, AND THERE'S AN OLE IN ME 'AT. AND I BET ME SIDEBURNS WON'T GROW BACK NEITHER. TELL THE PROF I WANT DAMAGES AND DANGER MONEY!

So you've been warned. Electricity can do shocking things to the human body. Oh, so you want to know more? Well, if you want to check out the gruesome details you can – just carry on reading...

SHOCK TREATMENT

Getting a massive surge of electricity running through your body is no picnic, as we've seen, but that didn't stop certain doctors using electricity to help people get better. Are you shocked? You will be. We'll be back after the commercial break...

ELECTRIC ADVERTS

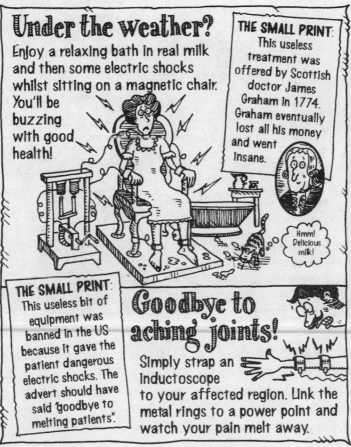

Under the weather?

Enjoy a relaxing bath in real milk and then some electric shocks whilst sitting on a magnetic chair. You'll be buzzing with good health!

THE SMALL PRINT: This useless treatment was offered by Scottish doctor James Graham in 1774. Graham eventually lost all his money and went insane.

Hmm! Delicious milk!

THE SMALL PRINT: This useless bit of equipment was banned in the US because it gave the patient dangerous electric shocks. The advert should have said 'goodbye to melting patients".

Goodbye to aching joints!

Simply strap an inductoscope to your affected region. Link the metal rings to a power point and watch your pain melt away.

241

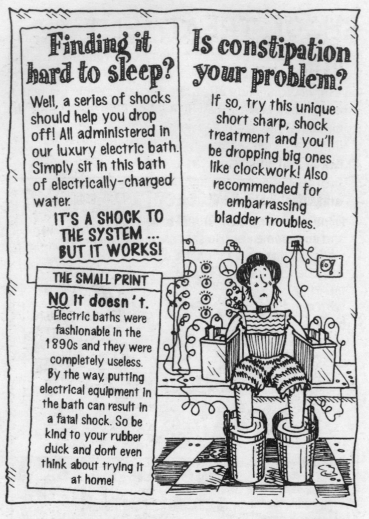

Finding it hard to sleep?

Well, a series of shocks should help you drop off! All administered in our luxury electric bath. Simply sit in this bath of electrically-charged water.

IT'S A SHOCK TO THE SYSTEM ... BUT IT WORKS!

THE SMALL PRINT

NO it doesn't. Electric baths were fashionable in the 1890s and they were completely useless. By the way, putting electrical equipment in the bath can result in a fatal shock. So be kind to your rubber duck and don't even think about trying it at home!

Is constipation your problem?

If so, try this unique short sharp, shock treatment and you'll be dropping big ones like clockwork! Also recommended for embarrassing bladder troubles.

Although it was about as useful as a pair of exploding underpants, all this primitive electric medicine is quite understandable, seeing as there is so much electricity in your body.

Oh yes there is...

242

Shocking electricity fact file

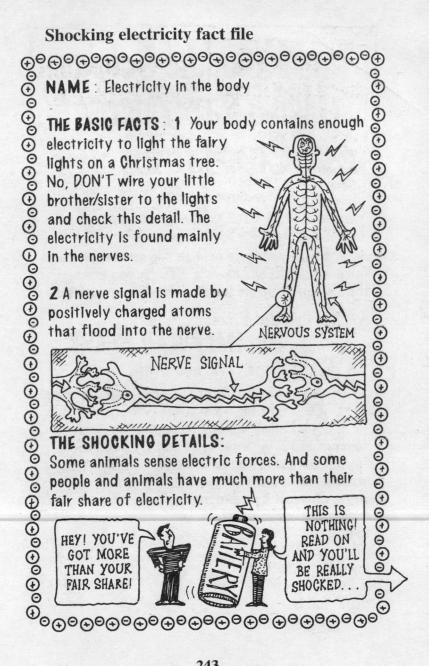

NAME: Electricity in the body

THE BASIC FACTS: **1** Your body contains enough electricity to light the fairy lights on a Christmas tree. No, DON'T wire your little brother/sister to the lights and check this detail. The electricity is found mainly in the nerves.

2 A nerve signal is made by positively charged atoms that flood into the nerve.

NERVOUS SYSTEM

NERVE SIGNAL

THE SHOCKING DETAILS:
Some animals sense electric forces. And some people and animals have much more than their fair share of electricity.

HEY! YOU'VE GOT MORE THAN YOUR FAIR SHARE!

BATTERY

THIS IS NOTHING! READ ON AND YOU'LL BE REALLY SHOCKED...

THE HORRIBLE SCIENCE LIVING ELECTRICITY COMPETITION

Class one - Nasty Nature

Yep, it's true that some animals can sense electrical forces – and the bad news is that this can make them vicious. Here are the most horrible examples...

3rd Prize:
HAMMERHEAD SHARK

Lives: Warm oceans

Sharks like the hammerhead can sense the electrical pulses in the nerves of their victims. To do this the hammerhead uses senses in its oddly-shaped bonce. But the shark is too good at its work because it also senses the electrical waves given off by submarine microphone cables (used to listen out for other subs) and attacks them! With shocking results ... for the shark that is.

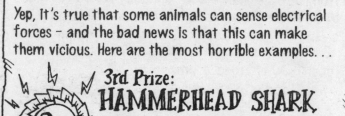

ERK!

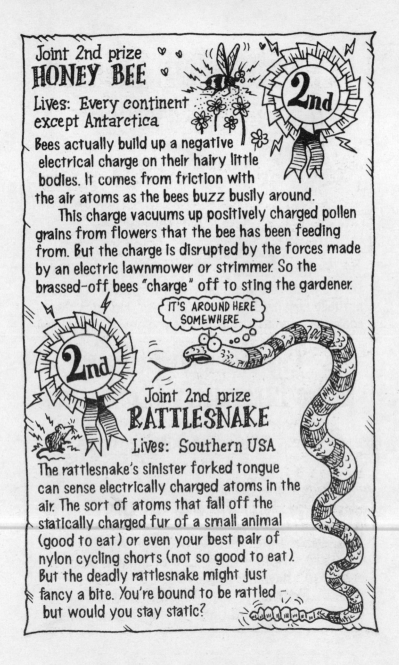

Joint 2nd prize
HONEY BEE

Lives: Every continent except Antarctica

Bees actually build up a negative electrical charge on their hairy little bodies. It comes from friction with the air atoms as the bees buzz busily around.

This charge vacuums up positively charged pollen grains from flowers that the bee has been feeding from. But the charge is disrupted by the forces made by an electric lawnmower or strimmer. So the brassed-off bees "charge" off to sting the gardener.

IT'S AROUND HERE SOMEWHERE

Joint 2nd prize
RATTLESNAKE

Lives: Southern USA

The rattlesnake's sinister forked tongue can sense electrically charged atoms in the air. The sort of atoms that fall off the statically charged fur of a small animal (good to eat) or even your best pair of nylon cycling shorts (not so good to eat). But the deadly rattlesnake might just fancy a bite. You're bound to be rattled – but would you stay static?

245

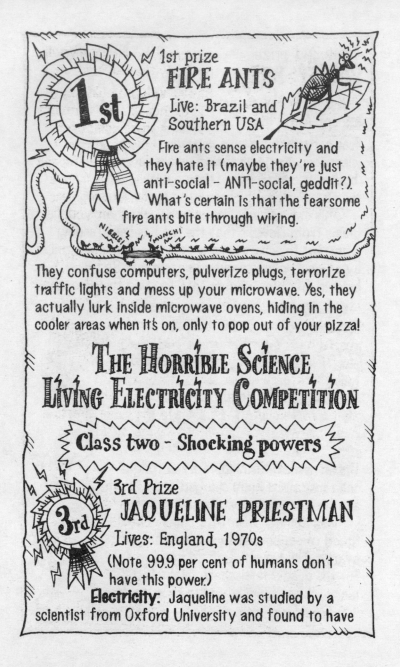

1st prize
FIRE ANTS

Live: Brazil and Southern USA

Fire ants sense electricity and they hate it (maybe they're just anti-social – ANTI-social, geddit?). What's certain is that the fearsome fire ants bite through wiring.

NIBBLE! MUNCHI

They confuse computers, pulverize plugs, terrorize traffic lights and mess up your microwave. Yes, they actually lurk inside microwave ovens, hiding in the cooler areas when it's on, only to pop out of your pizza!

THE HORRIBLE SCIENCE LIVING ELECTRICITY COMPETITION

Class two - Shocking powers

3rd Prize
JAQUELINE PRIESTMAN

Lives: England, 1970s

(Note 99.9 per cent of humans don't have this power.)

Electricity: Jaqueline was studied by a scientist from Oxford University and found to have

ARGH!

ten times more electricity in her body than normal.

Shock value: Could make TVs change channels without touching them and power sockets explode. For some unknown reason she stopped being electric when she ate green vegetables. So greens really are good for you!

2nd Prize
ELECTRIC CATFISH

2nd

Lives: African rivers

Electricity: Makes 350 volts in a special muscle just under its skin. The electricity is made by moving positively charged atoms to one end of its body. This causes an electrical current in the same way that a movement of electrons in the same direction makes an electrical current (see page 301).

Shock value: Enough power to kill a fish but that didn't stop the ancient Egyptians eating it. Would you risk an electric shock from your supper?

THE TASTE IS SHOCKING!

247

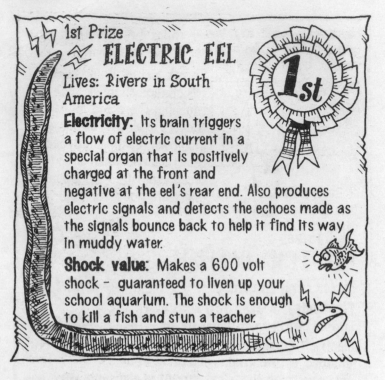

1st Prize

ELECTRIC EEL

1st

Lives: Rivers in South America

Electricity: Its brain triggers a flow of electric current in a special organ that is positively charged at the front and negative at the eel's rear end. Also produces electric signals and detects the echoes made as the signals bounce back to help it find its way in muddy water.

Shock value: Makes a 600 volt shock – guaranteed to liven up your school aquarium. The shock is enough to kill a fish and stun a teacher.

SOME SHOCKING FIRST AID

Imagine your teacher actually did suffer an electric shock. Would you know what to do? Well, you're about to find out...

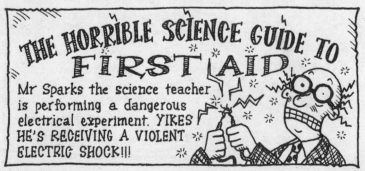

THE HORRIBLE SCIENCE GUIDE TO FIRST AID

Mr Sparks the science teacher is performing a dangerous electrical experiment. YIKES HE'S RECEIVING A VIOLENT ELECTRIC SHOCK!!!

Nasty! So what are you going to do to help? YES ... you've got to do *something*.

GULP!

CLICK!

ON
OFF

1 Switch off the power. If you touch Mr Sparks before you do this you might get an electric shock too.

2 Even now don't touch Mr Sparks – you might still get a shock. Use a rubber or wooden object such as a ruler to knock away the electric wire.

3 Send someone to ring for an ambulance. Mr Sparks will need complete rest and a check-up. Oh well, looks like you can go home early from school. And having saved his life, chances are he'll be so grateful he'll let you off homework for the rest of term. Yeah right, dream on....

HURRY!

Bet you never knew!
If the victim is holding the electrified object the muscles of their hand will squeeze so they can't let it go. According to one story a pop star was holding his microphone when it gave him a severe shock. He couldn't let it go and ended up on the floor yelling loudly. Everyone thought it was part of the act!

HAVE A HEART

The most important electrical charge in your body is the signal (similar to a nerve signal) that controls your heart beat. It's made by an area of muscle in the upper part of the heart. The signal makes the heart muscle squeeze in a regular rhythm.

HOPE I DON'T HAVE A POWERCUT!

SQUEEZE! PUMP!

Each squeeze pumps blood into and out of the heart sending it around the body and keeping us alive.

The heart can be monitored using a brilliant gizmo called the electrocardiogram (e-leck-tro-car-de-a-gram) developed by Dutch scientist Willem Einthoven (1860–1927) in 1903. Metal electrodes on the chest pick up electrical pulses from the nerve signals that control the heart. The pulses pass along a wire stretched between the poles of a magnet, making the wire bend very slightly. The machine displays this bending as a pattern on a screen.

But if this rhythm ever breaks down it's SERIOUSLY BAD NEWS. The condition is called ventricular fibrillation (ven-tric-ular fib-brill-la-tion). The heart flutters helplessly like an injured bird and stops pumping blood. The blood brings life-giving oxygen (a gas taken from the air by the lungs) to the body and without it the body will die in minutes. *And the shocking truth is that this terrifying condition can be triggered by an electric shock.*

Bet you never knew!
But the heart can be re-started. Incredibly, the best way is to give it an electric shock. Yes, you did read that right – another electric shock!

For reasons that scientists don't quite understand, the shock stops the fluttering of the heart so it can re-start itself. This fact was discovered in an especially tragic fashion. Read on for the heart-rending details...

STRAIGHT FROM THE HEART
Arizona, USA, 1947

"Here we have an interesting case. A 14-year-old male with a chest that hasn't grown properly for several years – making him unable to breathe normally. Am I going too fast?"

Top surgeon Claude Beck glanced at the medical students who were taking notes and, as usual, following his morning ward round like a flock of white-coated gulls after a fishing boat.

Beck had short greying hair, a square face, a square jaw and looked you squarely in the eye even when he had bad news to announce. And right now he was gazing straight into the eyes of his young patient.

"I wish I could tell you the op will be a cinch son, but it's an involved procedure. We've got to separate your ribs from your breastbone so you can breathe normally. Still I reckon we'll pull it off." Mickey's eyes were huge and dark and the rest of him looked thin and pale under his crew cut.

"And then?" he whispered anxiously.

"You'll be right as rain."

Mickey struggled to ask another question but he was short of breath and the surgeon and his students had already moved on. So later he asked a nurse about Dr Beck.

"Oh yes, Mickey," she smiled. "He's a real expert. Why, he's so clever he's even gone and developed a machine to re-start hearts using electric shocks. It's called a defibrillator. He's been testing it out on dogs. So don't you worry – you're in good hands."

Beck did indeed pull it off. The operation went just fine and after two hours the ribs were separated. The tricky part was over and the surgeon sighed with relief as he carefully sewed up the wound. Then, without warning Mickey's heart stopped beating. The unconscious boy gave a gentle sigh as his life ebbed away.

There was no time to think – and only seconds to act.

"Cardiac arrest!" yelled Beck, grabbing a scalpel and slicing through the stitches holding the side of the wound. There was just one thing he could do, one terrible option. He pulled aside the bone and muscle and grabbed the boy's heart. It was quivering like a hot bloody jelly.

"Ventricular fibrillation!" he snapped. Already he was gently squeezing the heart in his hands – willing it to start pumping blood on its own. Willing the boy to come back to life. For 35 minutes the surgeon frantically massaged the heart between shots of drugs designed to stimulate the muscle – but he knew that he was only buying time. There was just one hope.

"Fetch my defibrillator!" he ordered. "I'm going to try to shock the heart."

He glanced at the white, strained face of the anaesthetist. She was shaking her head.

"But," she protested. "It's never been tested on humans – only dogs."

"We've got to try it," said Beck desperately. "If not..."

The porter quickly wheeled Beck's machine, a mass of wires and dials, into the operating theatre and plugged it into the mains.

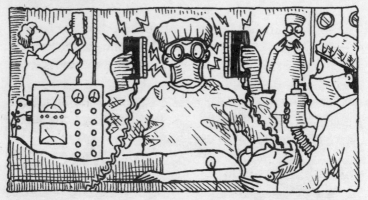

Beck placed the silver electric paddles to the boy's heart and fired 1,000 volts of electricity. The paddles jumped under Beck's hands but the heart was still, lifeless.

"We're losing him!" shouted the nurse.

Sweat ran down Beck's forehead and into his surgical mask. Once more he was frantically squeezing the slippery heart in his hands. Twenty-five agonising minutes passed, Beck's arms were aching but he dared not stop. More drugs were injected but still the heart would not beat. Perhaps it would be easier to let the boy die, Beck reasoned, knowing he could easily stop. But something drove him on.

"I'll try again," said the surgeon grimly, applying the paddles to the heart with shaking hands. Another jolt of electricity, longer this time, and 1,500 volts made the paddles jump.

There was a long tense silence.

"It's working!" said Beck, his voice hoarse with relief. The heart was pulsing and beating blood strongly and normally as if nothing had happened. And the nurses, the anaesthetist, the whole theatre staff broke into wild cheering.

Later that day Mickey was sitting up in bed.

"I'm starving," he complained. "The food here is shocking."

The nurse smiled, her eyes glistening with happiness and relief. "Well, Mickey," she said, "I think I can safely say we've all had a shocking time."

SHOCKING MEDICINE

1 Beck's defibrillator became a standard item of equipment in hospitals where it has saved tens of thousands of lives. Then, in 1960 US doctors developed a battery-powered version that could be used in ambulances. And today there are even small defibrillators that can be implanted inside the body. These fire tiny jolts of electricity into the heart if its rhythm breaks down.

2 The pacemaker is a similar device. Like an implanted defibrillator it runs off a battery outside the body but

255

unlike a defibrillator it produces regular shocks to keep the heart beating normally. In 1999 surgeons implanted a tiny pacemaker – the size of a 50 pence coin – to boost the heart of a three-week-old baby.

PACEMAKER

HIS NAPPY NEEDS CHANGING EVERY DAY BUT NOT HIS BATTERIES

3 In 1995 surgeons equipped a British woman with a battery-operated machine that helped her stand up. The woman's nerves had been damaged in a car accident and the machine fired electrical signals to her undamaged nerves to make her muscles move.

Have you spotted what these inventions have in common? No? Well, here's a clue – it's metal, it's full of chemicals and produces energy. No – it's not a can of fizzy drink! It's a battery, and without it most machines would be so much scrap metal. Well, by some shocking coincidence the next chapter's all about batteries – so why not read on? You can stretch yourself on the sofa and relax as you read. It's sure to re-charge your batteries – ha ha.

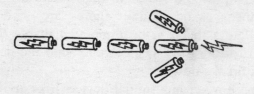

BULGING BATTERIES

Remember those kids on the Island of Horra? Bet they wished they'd brought a few batteries with them! Batteries are a great way of storing electricity so you take it with you and use it to power torches and radios and toy cars and walking, talking, crying, peeing dolls ... whatever you want. But how do they work?

TEACHER'S TEA-BREAK TEASER

All you need is a battery and a big grin. Knock on the staffroom door and when it creaks open hold up the battery.

Your teacher will probably say "It's a battery you little idiot!" Then you can shake your head sadly.

Yes, the correct name for a "battery" is a "dry cell". It's called that because the chemicals inside are in a paste and not in a liquid as they were in the first batteries, or cells. The word "battery" actually means a number of cells put together to make power, as in a torch. Anyway, we'll go on using "battery" in its everyday sense.

Shocking electricity fact file

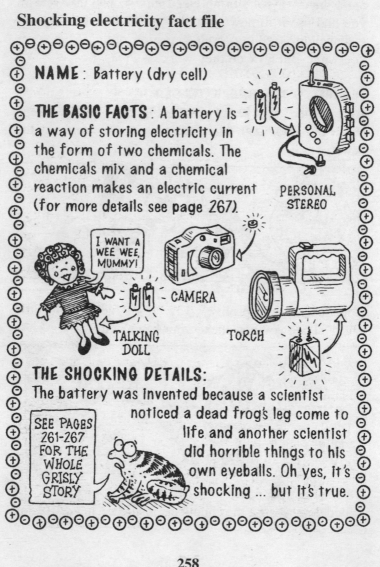

NAME: Battery (dry cell)

THE BASIC FACTS: A battery is a way of storing electricity in the form of two chemicals. The chemicals mix and a chemical reaction makes an electric current (for more details see page 267).

PERSONAL STEREO

I WANT A WEE WEE, MUMMY!

CAMERA

TALKING DOLL

TORCH

THE SHOCKING DETAILS:
The battery was invented because a scientist noticed a dead frog's leg come to life and another scientist did horrible things to his own eyeballs. Oh yes, it's shocking ... but it's true.

SEE PAGES 261-267 FOR THE WHOLE GRISLY STORY

Hall of Fame: Luigi Galvani (1737–1798) and Alessandro Volta (1745–1827)

Nationality: Italian

This is the story of two Italian scientists who started off as friends and ended up deadly enemies, and on the way both made major contributions to the science of electricity.

ALESSANDRO'S STORY...

The clever boy was educated by priests. His teachers were so impressed by him they tried to bribe him to train as a priest by giving him sweets.

But Alessandro's family didn't want their son to be a priest and took him away from school. (If only all families were so understanding!) Young Alessandro became interested in science and became a science teacher at Como and later a professor at Pavia University.

259

Alessandro got interested in electricity when he invented a pistol fired by an electric spark produced by static electricity. This set fire to methane gas contained in the pistol. Remember methane – it's the gas found in farts and rotting rubbish. And no, before you ask, you can't use exploding farts to shoot people.

Luigi's story

Young Galvani trained to be a doctor and later lectured in medicine at the University of Bologna whilst working as a doctor. He made a study of bones and later kidneys without making any startling discoveries.

But in the 1780s he became interested in nerves and made an electrifying breakthrough. Anyway, here are the letters that Luigi and his buddy Alessandro wrote to one another (beware, they could well be forgeries).

Bologna University 1780

MY METAL SCALPEL

Dear Aless,
You'll never guess what's happened! I was cutting up a frog's leg - as you know I'm researching nerves - and something shocking happened. There was a spark and the frog's leg twitched!

FROG'S LEG

METAL SHEET UNDERNEATH

Well, I checked and the frog was definitely dead. Oddly enough, the leg only seems to twitch if you touch it with metals. Bone or glass, for example, don't work. So I tried an experiment - I fixed some frog legs with brass hooks to the iron bars outside my lab windows and get this! The legs were all twitching merrily like a line of high-kicking dancers. The neighbour's cat got a real shock!

I think the frog's muscle contains electricity which forms a current through the metal. I think this electricity is the spark of life itself -

261

already some of my fellow scientists are trying to bring dead bodies back to life by giving them electric shocks – no success there I'm afraid! But I'm still really excited – in fact I'm galvanized. Nice word that!*

Your mate, Luigi

*A NOTE TO THE READER

Yes, the word "galvanized", meaning to get a sudden surge of energy, was inspired by Galvani's experiment. Well, as you can imagine, Volta was galvanized into making his own experiments...

Dear Luigi

That's a really interesting discovery but I'm sorry to say I don't think you're right about electricity in the body. First of all I gave an electric shock to a live frog. The frog trembled but it didn't jump. "Why not?" I asked myself. I decided to investigate whether electricity makes our senses work. So I gave my tongue and eyeballs and ears electric shocks to see if I started tasting, seeing and hearing things that weren't there. I didn't – and yeouch, it hurt!

Then suddenly I realized the shocking truth. I reckon it's the metals you used that made the electric current and it simply ran through the frog's leg and made it twitch. Since then I've actually managed to make electricity flow between two metals like this...

ONE BOWL CONTAINS A BAR OF ZINC

BARS LINKED BY WIRE. IF YOU TOUCH THE WIRE YOU GET AN ELECTRIC SHOCK.

ONE BOWL CONTAINS A BAR OF COPPER

TWO BOWLS OF SALTY WATER (I HAVE FOUND BY EXPERIMENT THAT THE ELECTRIC CURRENT TRAVELS MORE EASILY THROUGH SALTY WATER.)

So there you have it...
Your pal,
Alessandro →

SCIENTIFIC NOTE

1 Volta was right. Like any animal or human body the frog's leg was mostly salty water and electricity can travel through this mixture. But Galvani wasn't totally wrong – after all, the nerves do send a kind of electrical signal (check back to page 243 if you're not sure what I'm talking about).

2 Volta was right about his experiment too. Electrons flow from the zinc to the copper and this forms an electric current. But Galvani wasn't impressed.

Bologna University 1795

Dear Professor Volta,
How could you disagree with me like that! You really are re-Volta-ing TORTURING that poor little frog! At least I wait till they're dead!!! I'm still sure I'm right about animals making electricity. I mean look at electric catfish - they definitely make electricity don't they? Aha - gotcha there! Yah boo sucks to you!

Yours crossly
Galvani

YEAH!

Pavia University 1799

Dear Frog-features

You're wrong, wrong, WRONG! And what's more I can prove it! I was doing an experiment on senses. I put a metal coin on my tongue and another type of metal coin under my tongue and noticed a tingling and a disgusting taste. I was THRILLED! I realized the metals were producing electricity so I thought I'd make a machine to do this job – and PROVE YOU WRONG ONCE AND FOR ALL. I'm calling it my "Voltaic pile" – good name, eh?

Link a wire from the bottom to the top of the pile and you get electric sparks.

The more discs piled on each other the more power you get.

So there! You can take your frog's legs and hop it!

Volta

VOLTAIC PILE

ZINC DISC

COPPER DISC

CARDBOARD SOAKED IN SALTY WATER (TAKES THE PLACE OF MY TONGUE)

You!

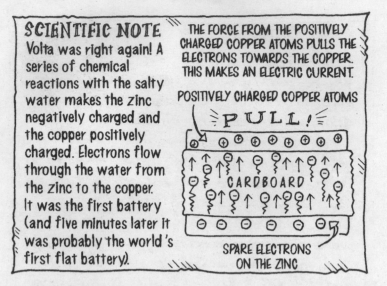

SCIENTIFIC NOTE
Volta was right again! A series of chemical reactions with the salty water makes the zinc negatively charged and the copper positively charged. Electrons flow through the water from the zinc to the copper. It was the first battery (and five minutes later it was probably the world's first flat battery).

THE FORCE FROM THE POSITIVELY CHARGED COPPER ATOMS PULLS THE ELECTRONS TOWARDS THE COPPER. THIS MAKES AN ELECTRIC CURRENT.

POSITIVELY CHARGED COPPER ATOMS

PULL!

CARDBOARD

SPARE ELECTRONS ON THE ZINC

WHAT HAPPENED IN THE END?

Galvani never gave up his idea and he never forgave Volta for disagreeing with him. He lost his job when the French Emperor Napoleon took over in Italy because he wouldn't support the French, and died a disappointed man. Volta got on well with the Emperor who made him a count and his invention made him famous. Today the volt, a unit that measures the amount of "pressure" behind electrons in an electric current, is named after him.

Bet you never knew!
The problem with Volta's invention is that the soggy cardboard kept drying up. The more familiar battery of today (the dry cell – remember?) was invented in 1866 by French inventor Georges Leclanché (1839–1882). It uses a mixture of chemicals to make chemical reactions that result in electrons flowing from the zinc inner container to the carbon rod.

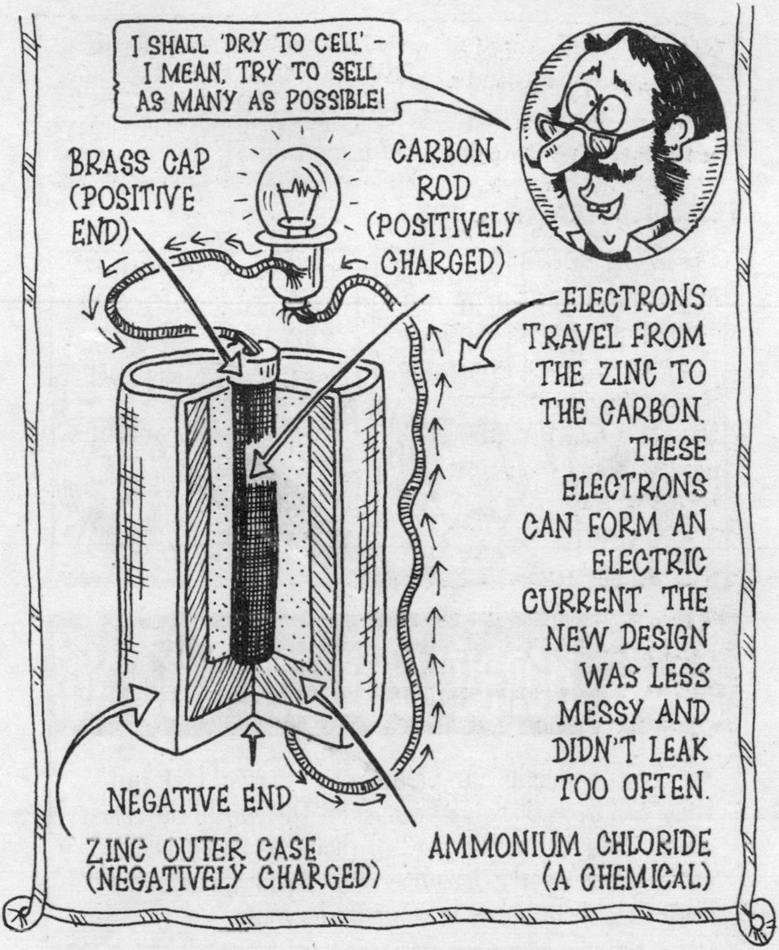

I SHALL 'DRY TO CELL' – I MEAN, TRY TO SELL AS MANY AS POSSIBLE!

BRASS CAP (POSITIVE END)

CARBON ROD (POSITIVELY CHARGED)

ELECTRONS TRAVEL FROM THE ZINC TO THE CARBON. THESE ELECTRONS CAN FORM AN ELECTRIC CURRENT. THE NEW DESIGN WAS LESS MESSY AND DIDN'T LEAK TOO OFTEN.

NEGATIVE END

ZINC OUTER CASE (NEGATIVELY CHARGED)

AMMONIUM CHLORIDE (A CHEMICAL)

COULD YOU BE A SCIENTIST?

Which way round do the batteries go in a torch? Yeah, OK you can try it out – or you could think about which way the electrons move. Is it…

a) Positively charged end to positively charged end?

b) Negatively charged end to negatively charged end?

c) Negatively charged end to positively charged end?

Answer: c) Remember that negative electrons flow towards positive atoms – so for electricity to flow and your torch to work you have to put the negative and positive ends together.

TERRIBLE TEACHER JOKE

WHAT DOES THE CHEMICAL SIGN NH₄CL STAND FOR?

IT'S ON THE TIP OF MY TONGUE.

IT'S AMMONIUM CHLORIDE AND IT'S POISONOUS SO YOU'D BETTER SPIT IT OUT!

HORRIBLE HEALTH WARNING!

Battery chemicals can be harmful. If they leak out they can even dissolve your skin! Throw old batteries away (and not in the fire) or recharge them. Never try cutting one open otherwise your burning curiosity might result in burns in your underwear.

BRILLIANT BATTERIES

The brilliant thing about batteries is that you can use them anywhere. On the beach and in the car and in the toilet. And there's plenty of choice of batteries each using different chemicals to produce electrons and make an electric current.

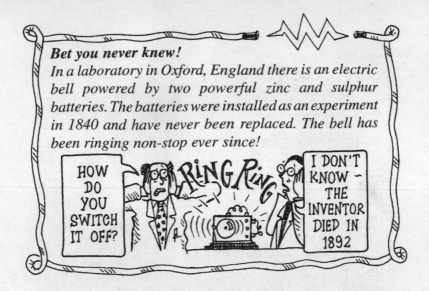

Bet you never knew!
In a laboratory in Oxford, England there is an electric bell powered by two powerful zinc and sulphur batteries. The batteries were installed as an experiment in 1840 and have never been replaced. The bell has been ringing non-stop ever since!

One of the most interesting battery-powered machines is the battery-powered car – no not a toy one, a real one. By the 2000s scientists were developing cool cars that could drive hundreds of km without a recharge. Japanese students even built one car that could zoom at 122 km (76 miles) per hour even though it was powered by ordinary AA batteries. Mind you, back in 1985 things were very different. A battery car was launched with massive hype. But was it more hype than horsepower?

▷ PEDAL HOME IF YOUR BATTERY FAILS!

▷ AT JUST 79 CM HIGH YOU CAN REALLY GET TO GRIPS WITH THE ROAD AND ENJOY THE THRILLS OF HUGE LORRIES MISSING YOU BY MILLIMETRES

THE SMALL PRINT

The Sinclair C5 company soon stopped trading. People were put off buying it for two reasons.

1 Safety fears.

2 They felt silly stuck in the middle of the road in something that looked like a kid's pedal car.

So there you have it, batteries are a great way to produce the electrical force to get things on the move. Even a Sinclair C5. But there's another kind of force too that's found in the C5's electric motors and indeed in any other electric motor.

And it's made by our old friends the electrons...

Wanna know more?

Well, read on, you're bound to feel drawn to the next chapter. It's mysteriously attractive ... just like a magnet!

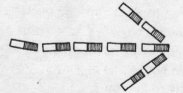

MYSTERIOUS MAGNETISM

Are you finding this book hard to put down? I expect it's the magnetic force coming from these pages. If you can *force* yourself to read the next few pages you'll find out what magnetism is and how it's made. Let's face a few facts...

Shocking electricity fact file

NAME: Magnetism

THE BASIC FACTS: **1** Magnetism is made by magnets. (Well, knock me over with a feather duster!)

2 What we call magnetism is actually the same force as the electric force made by electrons – that's why the posh scientific name for the force is electromagnetism (e-leck-tro-magnetism).

MAGNET

FORCE MADE BY ELECTRONS

REMEMBER THIS ON PAGE 41?

3 What this means is that every atom which has electrons is very slightly magnetic.

THE SHOCKING DETAILS:

QUESTION: But if atoms are magnetic and atoms are everywhere then how come everything isn't magnetic? How come you're not stuck to your bed in the morning? (No you're not, it just *feels* like you are.)

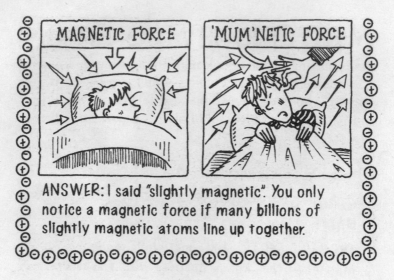

ANSWER: I said "slightly magnetic". You only notice a magnetic force if many billions of slightly magnetic atoms line up together.

MAGNETISM: THE INSIDE STORY

So how do you line up all those atoms? I mean, you'd need a tiny pair of tweezers and loads of patience and it would still take for ever.

THERE'S GOT TO BE AN EASIER WAY...

Well, you'll be pleased to know that inside a magnet this lining up is done quite naturally by those nice helpful atoms.

1 Inside a magnet the atoms line up to form little boxes (about 0.1 mm across) called domains (doe-mains). Inside these boxes the electrons can combine their forces to make what we call a magnetic force.

2 A magnet has two ends called north and south poles.

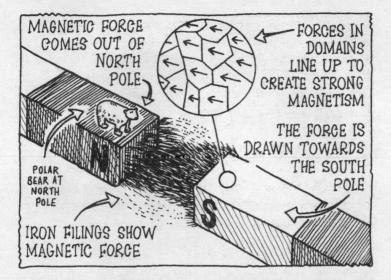

MAGNETIC FORCE COMES OUT OF NORTH POLE

FORCES IN DOMAINS LINE UP TO CREATE STRONG MAGNETISM

THE FORCE IS DRAWN TOWARDS THE SOUTH POLE

POLAR BEAR AT NORTH POLE

IRON FILINGS SHOW MAGNETIC FORCE

Dare you discover ... how to make a magnetic plane?

You will need:

A piece of tissue paper 2 cm x 1 cm

Sticky tape and scissors

A metal pin

A magnet (This should be as strong as possible – you could use several magnets in a line.)

A piece of thread 30 cm long.

What you do:

1 Thread the pin through the paper so it looks like a little plane (the paper being the wing).

2 Tie the string to the head of the pin.

3 Tape the end of the string to the side of a table.

4 Move the magnet near to the plane and try to make it fly without touching it.

What do you notice?

a) If I move the magnet away from the plane it stays flying.

b) The closer the magnet is to the plane the better it flies.

c) The magnet will only work if it's a certain way round.

Answer: b) The closer you are to the magnet the stronger its force. The area around a magnet that is affected by its force is called a "magnetic field". (Mind you, don't tread in any magnetic cow pats!)

Dare you discover ... if magnetism works underwater?

(No, you don't need a diving suit for this experiment.)

You will need:
A glass of water
A magnet
A paper clip

What you do:
1 Plop the paper clip in the water.

2 Place the magnet up against the *outside* of the glass.

3 Now try to use the magnet to bring the paper clip to the top of the glass without touching the paper clip and without getting the magnet wet.

What do you notice?

a) It's easy.

b) I can't move the paper clip at all.

c) The paper clip only moves when I hold the magnet *over* the water. This proves that magnetism works through water but not through glass.

Answer: a) This proves that magnetism works through glass and water.

Dare you discover ... how magnetic tape works?

Did you know that tape recorders work using magnetism? Yes, it's true. To find out more try this fascinating experiment.

You will need:

A cassette tape
A cassette recorder and microphone
A magnet

What you do:

1 Talk into the microphone. No, it doesn't really matter what you say – why not try a few farmyard impressions?

2 OK, that's enough farmyard impressions – I said THAT'S ENOUGH FARMYARD IMPRESSIONS!

Now rewind and play the tape. Rewind the tape and stop in the middle of your recording.

3 Now sweep the magnet across the tape four times.

4 Rewind and play the tape.

What do you notice?

a) My voice blanks out in the middle. My lovely recording is ruined!

b) The tape is LOUDER than ever and all the neighbours are complaining.

c) My voice sounds like an alien's.

Answer: a) The microphone turns your voice into electronic pulses and these are turned by a magnet into magnetic signals that rearrange the tiny bits of metal chemical on the tape to make a recording. Easy-peasey! Your magnet muddled up these chemicals so that the tape recording was lost.

HORRIBLE HEALTH WARNING!

Don't you DARE even *think* of using your mum and dad's classic tape collection for this experiment! Oh I see, it's too late. Well beware – your parents might use a magnet to grab your pocket money.

MAGNETIC QUIZ

1 Some Canadian coins are magnetic. TRUE/FALSE

2 Magnetism can be used to suck out diseased parts of bone marrow (the juicy pink bit that dogs love). TRUE/FALSE

3 An ultra-powerful magnet can pull the eyeballs out of your head. TRUE/FALSE

4 Magnetism stores information in computers. TRUE/FALSE

5 In Siberia people fish by chucking iron filings into lakes. When the fish have eaten the filings they are caught using magnets. TRUE/FALSE

6 There's a magnet inside your school bell and/or your school fire bell. TRUE/FALSE

7 Magnetism can power a full-sized train. TRUE/FALSE

Answers:

1 True. Canadian dimes are made of nickel – a metal that can be naturally magnetic.

2 True. In the mid-1980s British scientists discovered how to treat lumps of diseased bone marrow inside bones with chemicals coated in magnetic material. The chemicals stuck to the affected areas inside the bone. It was then possible to draw the diseased lumps out in tiny bits using powerful magnets. Hungry yet, Fido?

3 False. Human eyeballs aren't magnetic but magnets *are* used to remove tiny bits of metal from eyeballs after accidents.

4 True. For example, a floppy disk stores computer code like a tape recording as magnetic chemicals on its surface. The "read" head of the computer turns magnetic pulses from the disk into electric signals inside the computer. The hard disk is a series of magnetic disks that store information.

5 False.

6 True. The ringing that wakes you up at the end of a science lesson is made by a hammer hitting a bell. The hammer is yanked by a powerful magnet in the bell that responds to an electric current set up when someone presses the button.

7 True. In the 1990s Maglev trains were built in Japan and Germany. The train is lifted off the rail using powerful magnets. As the train glides forward, powerful magnets on board make electrons move in the reaction rail underneath the train. This creates an electric current which gives off a magnetic force that pulls the train forward. Fancy one for Christmas?

Maglev technology has also been used to make lifts and some really cool theme park white knuckle rides. With a bit of luck you could persuade your parents to let you go on one for your science homework. Well, you can only ask.

A FORCEFUL TALE

Magnets have a long history. About 2500 BC, according to legend, a Chinese Emperor guided his army through fog using a rock containing magnetite (also called lodestone). Well, stone me. He probably used a sliver of the rock hung from a thread.

Magnetite is naturally magnetic so a sliver of it points towards the north and can be used to make a compass, a device described by Chinese scientist and astronomer Shen Kuo (1030–1093) in 1088.

Chinese sailors used the compass to steer a course at sea, a technique that spread to Europe and the Middle East within 100 years. But although sailors happily used compasses, no one bothered to do experiments with magnets until a doctor called William Gilbert (1540–1603) came on the scene.

WONDERING WILLIAM

Little is known about William's early life. But he studied medicine and eventually became Royal Doctor to Queen Elizabeth of England.

HOW IS YOUR ROYAL ILLNESS - I MEAN HIGHNESS?

But just two years later the Queen died, so William's medicines must have been a dead loss. Anyway, he was the first person to investigate magnets in a scientific way. For example, people thought that if you rubbed a magnet with garlic the pong would drive the magnetism away. (Sounds reasonable – after all it can have this effect on your friends.) But Gilbert found the treatment didn't work.

THIS EXPERIMENT STINKS!

MY RESULTS ARE NOT TO BE SNIFFED AT

Gilbert was fascinated by the way that a magnetic compass pointed north and wanted to know why. At last he realized that the whole Earth is a magnet! He found this out by putting a magnetic compass needle on a small rod. The needle pointed north of course but it also dipped slightly downwards. This suggested that magnetism must come out of the Earth at some point far to the north and Gilbert reckoned (rightly) that the Earth itself is a GIANT magnet. I guess that's one magnet that would be too big for your fridge.

FIVE MAGNETIC EARTH FACTS

1 A sea of melted metal surrounds the Earth's core. If you fancied a dip you'd be crushed and burnt – but fortunately no human has ventured this deep.

2 Currents swirl around in the metal and the huge masses of electrons set up powerful electric and magnetic forces.

3 The magnetic forces come out of the ground at the South Magnetic pole, sweep round the Earth and enter the ground at the North Magnetic Pole.

4 Yes, you did read that right – it's the *opposite* of an ordinary magnet! In line with other magnets we really ought to say that the North Magnetic Pole is near the South Pole and the South Magnetic Pole is near the North Pole – that would bamboozle your Geography teacher! The reason for the confusion is that the north pole of a compass magnet happened to get its name because it points towards the North Magnetic Pole, which is towards the geographic south. Lost yet? You will be.

5 The direction of the magnetic force has flipped round about 300 times in the last 4,600 million years. (Don't ask me why or when it will happen next – no one knows!) This would make a compass needle point south instead of north and if it happened on a school trip you're bound to get lost. And then your teacher would really flip!

Talking about expeditions – d'you fancy a holiday?

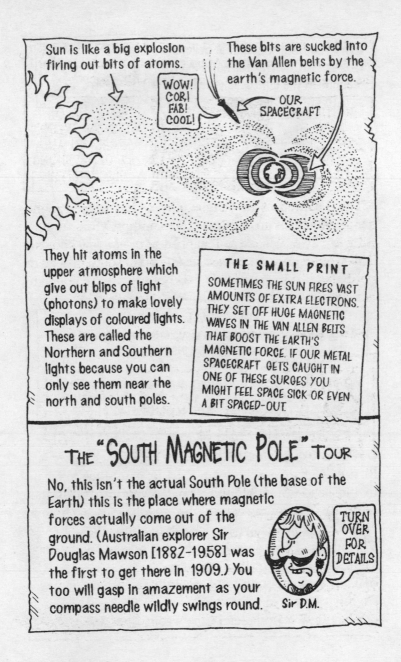

Sun is like a big explosion firing out bits of atoms.

WOW! COR! FAB! COOL!

These bits are sucked into the Van Allen belts by the earth's magnetic force.

OUR SPACECRAFT

They hit atoms in the upper atmosphere which give out blips of light (photons) to make lovely displays of coloured lights. These are called the Northern and Southern lights because you can only see them near the north and south poles.

THE SMALL PRINT

SOMETIMES THE SUN FIRES VAST AMOUNTS OF EXTRA ELECTRONS. THEY SET OFF HUGE MAGNETIC WAVES IN THE VAN ALLEN BELTS THAT BOOST THE EARTH'S MAGNETIC FORCE. IF OUR METAL SPACECRAFT GETS CAUGHT IN ONE OF THESE SURGES YOU MIGHT FEEL SPACE SICK OR EVEN A BIT SPACED-OUT.

THE "SOUTH MAGNETIC POLE" TOUR

No, this isn't the actual South Pole (the base of the Earth) this is the place where magnetic forces actually come out of the ground. (Australian explorer Sir Douglas Mawson [1882–1958] was the first to get there in 1909.) You too will gasp in amazement as your compass needle wildly swings round.

TURN OVER FOR DETAILS

Sir D.M.

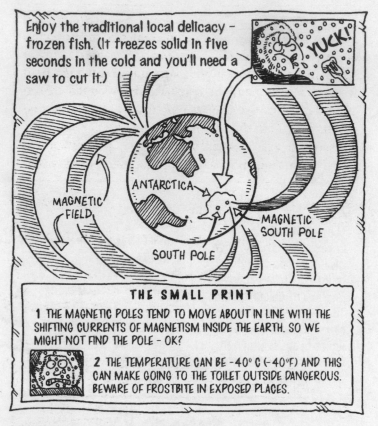

Enjoy the traditional local delicacy – frozen fish. (It freezes solid in five seconds in the cold and you'll need a saw to cut it.)

YUCK!

MAGNETIC FIELD

ANTARCTICA

MAGNETIC SOUTH POLE

SOUTH POLE

THE SMALL PRINT

1 THE MAGNETIC POLES TEND TO MOVE ABOUT IN LINE WITH THE SHIFTING CURRENTS OF MAGNETISM INSIDE THE EARTH. SO WE MIGHT NOT FIND THE POLE – OK?

2 THE TEMPERATURE CAN BE –40° C (–40°F) AND THIS CAN MAKE GOING TO THE TOILET OUTSIDE DANGEROUS. BEWARE OF FROSTBITE IN EXPOSED PLACES.

COULD YOU BE A SCIENTIST?

In 1995 American scientist Robert Beason stuck magnets to the heads of bobolinks (small American birds that normally fly south-east in the autumn). Beason then opened the birds' cages. What did the birds do?

a) Nothing. Their poor little magnetic heads were stuck to the metal floor of their cages.

b) They flew in roughly the right direction but they were slightly off course.

c) They flew in completely the wrong direction.

Answer: c) Scientists think that birds have tiny specks of magnetite in their brains that act like compasses. With the added magnets mucking up their system, the bobolinks were well and truly lost. Birds such as brown pelicans have weaker magnets at the back of their eyeballs which affect the way that their eyeballs react to light to see colour. The pelicans can see the direction of magnetic north as a colour spot like an after-image.

Bet you never knew!
You can destroy the power of a magnet by "killing" it – that's the actual word scientists use. It sounds rather sinister, like some dreadful murder. Well, if it was a crime would you know how to solve it?

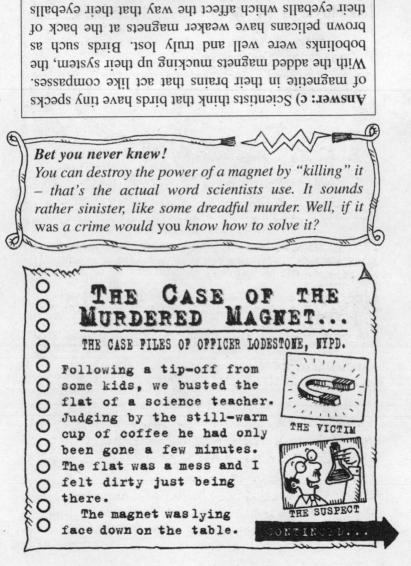

THE CASE OF THE MURDERED MAGNET...

THE CASE FILES OF OFFICER LODESTONE, NYPD.

Following a tip-off from some kids, we busted the flat of a science teacher. Judging by the still-warm cup of coffee he had only been gone a few minutes. The flat was a mess and I felt dirty just being there.

The magnet was lying face down on the table.

THE VICTIM

THE SUSPECT

CONTINUED...

285

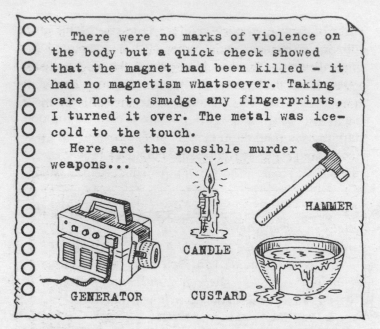

There were no marks of violence on the body but a quick check showed that the magnet had been killed — it had no magnetism whatsoever. Taking care not to smudge any fingerprints, I turned it over. The metal was ice-cold to the touch.

Here are the possible murder weapons...

CANDLE

HAMMER

GENERATOR

CUSTARD

Your mission ... is to find out how the magnet was killed. *Was it by...*

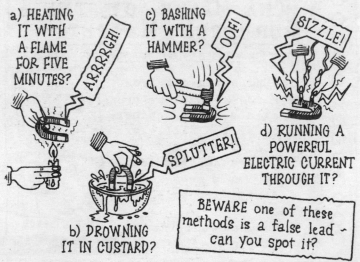

a) HEATING IT WITH A FLAME FOR FIVE MINUTES?

ARRRRGH!

c) BASHING IT WITH A HAMMER?

OOF!

SIZZLE!

d) RUNNING A POWERFUL ELECTRIC CURRENT THROUGH IT?

SPLUTTER!

b) DROWNING IT IN CUSTARD?

BEWARE one of these methods is a false lead - can you spot it?

Three of these methods would rearrange the atoms in the domains so the magnetic forces no longer pointed in a single direction. This would mean that the magnet lost its power. Read the case notes again ... you may find some more clues. OK – ready for this? The answer is **d)** and **b)** is useless!

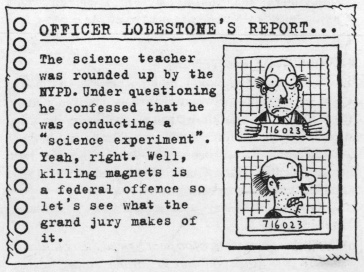

OFFICER LODESTONE'S REPORT...

The science teacher was rounded up by the NYPD. Under questioning he confessed that he was conducting a "science experiment". Yeah, right. Well, killing magnets is a federal offence so let's see what the grand jury makes of it.

716023

716023

What's that? Did you say "It doesn't sound too serious to me"? WELL, IT IS!!! You can't just go around killing magnets because magnets are vital and important. Vital to make THE MOST IMPORTANT MACHINE ON THE PLANET. A machine that literally powers the modern world. Wanna know more?

Well, why not "motor" on to the next chapter?

MIGHTY MAGNETIC MOTORS

Clean, silent, powerful. Electric motors power all sorts of things from washing machines to milk floats and the only time anyone notices them is when one doesn't work or gives their owners a nasty shock. But did you know that electric motors depend on magnetism and electricity working together?

A CURRENT OF EXCITEMENT

Before anyone could build a motor, scientists first had to figure out the link between electricity and magnetism. Yes, I know that you know that magnetism is the same force as the electric force made by electrons, but in those days electrons hadn't been discovered. Then in 1820 Danish scientist Hans Christian Oersted (1771–1851) stumbled across a connection.

Bet you never knew!
Christian's parents were too poor to feed their children so they gave Christian and his brother away to the neighbours. (No, your parents are unlikely to give your brother/sister to the folk next door so stop daydreaming and get on with this book.) But the boys managed to educate themselves from books. They did so well they were allowed into Copenhagen University, where Hans became a Professor.

Anyway, Hans wondered if an electric current had any effect on a compass needle. One day during a lecture he placed a compass needle near a fixed electric wire. The needle mysteriously swung away from the wire as if pushed by an invisible finger.

Oersted wasn't quite sure why this was happening but realized he'd stumbled across something really IMPORTANT.

COULD YOU BE A SCIENTIST?

You've been reading this book (unlike poor Oersted) so you can work out what was going on. What was it?

a) The electric force given out by the wire was pulling the magnetic compass needle towards it.

b) The force given out by the electrons in the wire was pushing the magnetic compass needle away.

c) The compass needle was moving as a result of static electricity.

Answer: b) The electric force is also a magnetic force – that's why it's called electromagnetism (remember that word from page 271?). And the forces made by electrons push against each other – remember that too? Well, the two forces pushed against each other as usual. This had the effect of pushing the compass needle away. (The wire would have moved too if it wasn't fixed.)

So the force from an electric current can make a magnet move and, as you're about to find out, this is exactly the principle behind an electric motor. Wanna know more?

Shocking electricity fact file

NAME : Electric motor

THE BASIC FACTS : **1** Every type of electric motor uses the electromagnetic force to make a wire loop move. Here's how...

LOOPY
INVENTION

WIRE
LOOP
TURNS

BATTERY

MAGNET

2 The electromagnetic forces in the wire and the magnets keep pushing against each other and this pushes the wire loop round.

3 The moving loop can be used to power the moving parts of a machine and keep it "ticking over".

THE SHOCKING DETAILS: You'll find electric motors in loads of things ... like an electric saw for cutting the tops of dead people's heads off so scientists can study their brains.

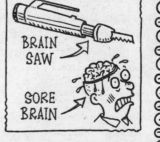

BRAIN
SAW

SORE
BRAIN

THE MOTOR RACE

The race was on to combine electricity and magnetism to make a working electric motor. But the basic idea was thought up in 1821 by scientist Michael Faraday (1791–1867). Faraday actually built a machine to show this and it was the first ever electric motor. In a first for *Horrible Science* we've actually persuaded the great scientist to explain how it works. (This is quite amazing since he's been dead for well over 100 years.)

DEAD BRAINY: MICHAEL FARADAY

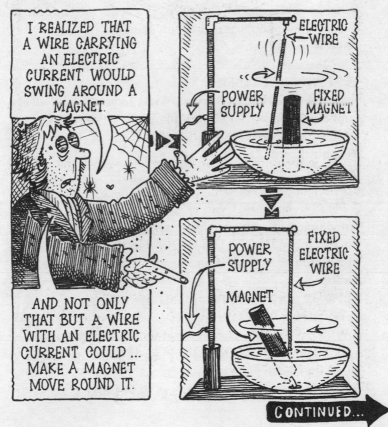

I REALIZED THAT A WIRE CARRYING AN ELECTRIC CURRENT WOULD SWING AROUND A MAGNET.

ELECTRIC WIRE

POWER SUPPLY

FIXED MAGNET

AND NOT ONLY THAT BUT A WIRE WITH AN ELECTRIC CURRENT COULD ... MAKE A MAGNET MOVE ROUND IT.

POWER SUPPLY

FIXED ELECTRIC WIRE

MAGNET

CONTINUED...

291

IN EACH CASE THE MOVEMENT IS DUE TO THE ELECTROMAGNETIC FORCES FROM THE WIRE AND MAGNET PUSHING AGAINST EACH OTHER. OF COURSE, IF YOU TOUCH THE WIRE YOU'LL GET A NASTY SHOCK...

ARGH! I NEARLY KILLED MYSELF!

M.F. HAS FORGOTTEN THAT HE'S BEEN DEAD FOR OVER 100 YEARS

What an achievement! Surely your teacher will be able to tell you more about this brilliant scientist.

Well *surely*?

TEST YOUR TEACHER

Special note – this is a very easy test so you should award your teacher a MINUS mark for every *wrong* answer.

1 What did Faraday's dad do? Was he...

a) A blacksmith?

b) An ice-cream seller?

c) A science teacher?

2 Faraday began his career as a bookbinder's assistant but landed a job as lab assistant to top scientist Sir Humphry Davy (1778–1829). How did he do it?

a) Sir Humphry sacked one of his assistants and created a vacancy.

b) Faraday bribed Davy with his life savings.

c) He got recommended by his science teacher.

3 Why did Sir Humphry quarrel with Faraday?

a) Sir Humphry accused Faraday of stealing his ideas about the electric motor.

b) Faraday borrowed his pen and didn't give it back.

c) Sir Humphry was jealous because Faraday was a better teacher than he was.

4 What was Faraday's favourite hobby?

a) Work – especially setting up science experiments.

b) Going to parties.

c) Teaching children about science.

5 Other scientists made machines based on Faraday's work but found it hard to make them work. What did Faraday do?

a) Made copies of the machine and sent it to them.

b) Wrote them rude letters with the word IDIOT scrawled in big letters.

c) Organized a special training day for them.

6 As an old man what problem did Faraday suffer from?

a) A weak memory.

b) Embarrassing hairy ears.

c) He lost his voice so he had to give up teaching.

7 When the Chancellor of the Exchequer came to Faraday's lab and asked what use electricity was how did Faraday reply?

Answers: All the answers are **a)** so it should be easy enough to add up your teacher's score.

1 Faraday's dad was always ill and the family was very poor.

2 Faraday had already got a job as a secretary after giving Davy a beautiful handmade book of notes on Davy's lectures. Yes, producing marvellous homework does pay off sometimes.

3 Like many scientists Davy was very sensitive about who gets the glory for discoveries. Davy and his scientist pal William Hyde Wollaston (1766–1828) had worked on a motor that didn't work. Faraday had benefited from their ideas but hadn't mentioned them when he wrote about his discovery.

4 Faraday had few friends and no social life. But he wasn't sad – he was a genius. Obviously, your teacher has no such excuse. You can award half a mark for **c)** because Faraday enjoyed teaching at the Royal Institution where he worked and even set up Christmas lectures for children.

5 That's the kind of man he was.

6 This came after an illness in 1839 that Faraday said affected his head. It might have been poisoning by the chemicals he used for experiments.

7 And sure enough in 1994 the British government plonked Value Added Tax on electricity.

What your teacher's score means

-7–0 Your teacher's ignorance is SHOCKING. Order them to take the rest of the term off in study leave. Oh well, you'll just have to amuse yourself in science lessons.

1–3 Passable. Could do better.

4–7 Check your teacher's drawer for a copy of this book. If you find one disqualify your teacher AT ONCE! By the way, if your teacher keeps saying **c)** she is totally absorbed in her job and needs a nice long holiday. Of course, you'll have to take one too.

Bet you never knew!

All Faraday's motor did was run around in circles and not do any work. Do you know anyone like that? The first working electric motor was made by Joseph Henry (1797–1878) in 1831. Henry was another remarkable scientist. He started his career as a watchmaker and then wrote plays before getting interested in science. He was not a greedy man and when he got a science job working for the Smithsonian Institute he refused a pay rise for 32 years.

IF YOU DON'T STOP TRYING TO GIVE ME A PAY RISE...I'LL GO ON STRIKE!

Dare you discover ... how to make your own electric motor?

You will need:

A compass OR a needle
A magnet
A 25-cm length of thread
Some Blu-Tack
Sticky tape
A 1.5-volt battery (HP11)
A piece of kitchen foil 28 cm x 6 cm
A grown-up to help. (Yes, they have their uses.)

What you do:

1 If you don't have a compass, stroke the needle with the magnet 30 times. This turns the needle into a magnet too.

2 Secure the needle to the end of the thread with a small blob of Blu-Tack in the middle so it hangs sideways in the air.

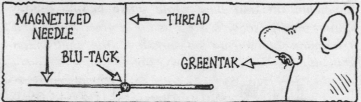

3 Stick the other end of the thread to a table top with more Blu-Tack.

4 Fold the foil in half lengthways and then fold it again lengthways. Make sure you don't tear the foil.

5 Use sticky tape to stick one end of the foil to the positive end of the battery and the other end to the negative end. This makes a circuit for an electric current to run through.

6 Now, EITHER ... hold the battery horizontal and pass the foil loop from side to side over the face of the compass.

OR put the foil loop round the needle and move the foil up and down without touching it.

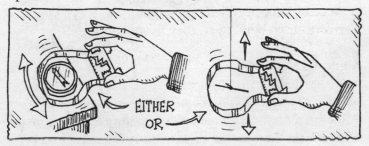

What do you notice?

a) The needle starts to glow with a strange blue light.

b) The needle twists round.

c) The needle jumps up and down.

> **Answer: b)** The compass needle turns round and round and the needle twists around. Either way the magnetic field produced by the wire moves with the wire. This keeps pushing away and then attracting the magnetic needle – just like a real electric motor!

SPOT THE ELECTRIC MOTOR QUIZ

Which of the household objects on the next page contains an electric motor? (No, you're NOT allowed to take them apart to find out.) Here's a clue instead – if it's got moving parts it's got an electric motor.

Answer: All of them!

Just take a look at this...

1 Ever wondered why fridges hum sometimes? (NO, it's not 'cos they're happy.) Specially cooled chemicals are pumped around pipes at the back that pass into the fridge and freezer areas.

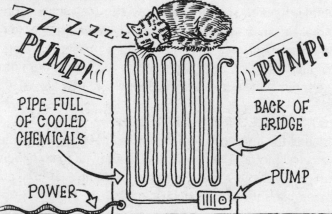

2 In a microwave oven the food goes round on a turntable driven by an electric motor.

The motor also drives the fan that is used to reflect microwaves on to the food.

3 The CD player uses a laser beam to scan tiny pits on the underside of the CD. The laser beam jumps lightly as it scans the pits producing a reflected flickering pattern that the CD player turns into electric pulses that an amplifier can turn into sounds. Got all that? Well, the laser couldn't scan anything if the CD wasn't spinning and this is powered by an electric motor.

4 The DVD player is a bit like a CD player – only for sound AND images such as your favourite movies. Once again you need a electric motor to spin the disc so that it can be scanned by a laser beam.

5 A hairdryer is simply a coil of wire that heats up by friction as electrons crush through it (just like a light bulb – see page 181).

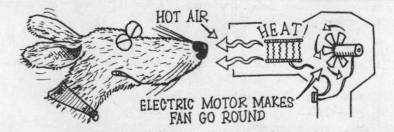

Mind you, an electric motor is pretty useless without an electric current to power it. And although you can make a current with a battery and some wire, if you want electricity on tap day and night you really need a more powerful current – so let's look at some shocking currents.

No, I mean *electric* currents... Amazingly enough, people have argued and died over the best way to make an electric current.

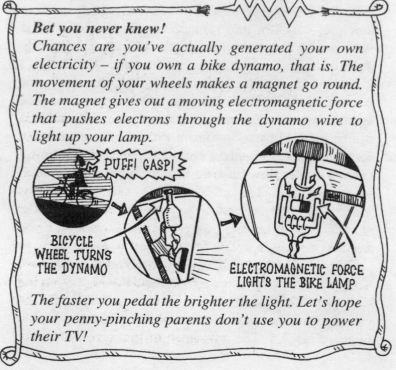

Bet you never knew!
Chances are you've actually generated your own electricity – if you own a bike dynamo, that is. The movement of your wheels makes a magnet go round. The magnet gives out a moving electromagnetic force that pushes electrons through the dynamo wire to light up your lamp.

PUFF! GASP!

BICYCLE WHEEL TURNS THE DYNAMO

ELECTROMAGNETIC FORCE LIGHTS THE BIKE LAMP

The faster you pedal the brighter the light. Let's hope your penny-pinching parents don't use you to power their TV!

Bet you never knew!

The first town in Britain to have its own electricity supply was Godalming in Surrey. But the project set up in 1880 was a flop because few people wanted the upheaval of having the new-fangled wires put into their homes. A second power station built in London a few months later proved more successful.

HIGH POWER - HIGH STAKES

Soon power generation became big business. And when electric power was launched in America in the 1880s the stakes were very high indeed. Leading the way were two power-hungry tycoons, Thomas Edison (1847–1931) and George Westinghouse (1846–1914).

Edison was a wealthy inventor with a multi-million-dollar power business complete with 121 power stations. He championed **direct current**, which means the electric current simply flows along a wire from the power station to your house. The problem was that the electrons gradually escaped through the wires so that the power stations had to be built quite close to houses and you needed one power station for each part of town.

George Westinghouse backed **alternating current**. The power station pumped out a current that kept changing direction. This made shock waves rush through the electrons in the wire at 300,000 kilometres (186,000 miles) a second. The advantage of this type of current was that it could be boosted using a device called a transformer and pumped into the wires at a massive 500,000 volts. And although electrons still leaked out of the wires there were more than enough to be carried long distances. At the other end of the wires a second transformer simply reduced the power to a safer level.

Westinghouse planned to take over Edison's business empire. But Edison insisted that alternating current was dangerous. Things were about to turn nasty ... shockingly nasty...

CRUEL CURRENTS

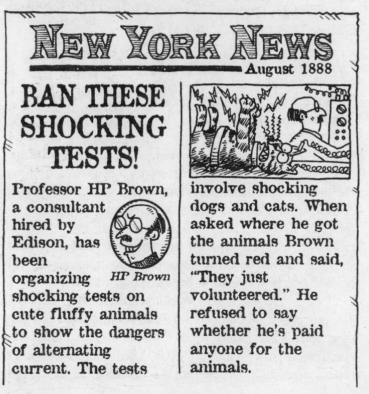

NEW YORK NEWS
August 1888

BAN THESE SHOCKING TESTS!

Professor HP Brown, a consultant hired by Edison, has been organizing *HP Brown* shocking tests on cute fluffy animals to show the dangers of alternating current. The tests involve shocking dogs and cats. When asked where he got the animals Brown turned red and said, "They just volunteered." He refused to say whether he's paid anyone for the animals.

STOP PRESS!

There have been a number of pet cats and dogs disappearing lately and the local kids seem to have more pocket money than usual.

NEW YORK NEWS

December 1888

A SHOCKING WAY TO GO!

New York State is to execute murderers. This follows embarrassing incidents when hangings have gone wrong and people have had their heads pulled off by the rope. The first victim to be electrocuted is to be William Kemplar a fruitseller convicted of killing his girlfriend. Thomas Edison says the execution will prove the danger of alternating current.

W. Kemplar (before the murder)

STOP PRESS!

Westinghouse is shocked that his alternating current is going to be used to kill someone. Kemplar says he's shocked too and he's appealing, claiming the execution is too cruel. We expect him to be even more shocked if the execution goes ahead.

W. Kemplar (Yesterday)

NEW YORK NEWS

A DEAD LOSS

Kemplar is dead. His appeal was rejected after Thomas Edison claimed that electrocution wasn't such a bad way to go, because it kills nice and quickly. But the execution in the newly-designed electric chair went horribly wrong. Kemplar survived the first shock and took another jolt of over a minute resulting in smoke and sparks coming out of his body. The execution was a shocking sight

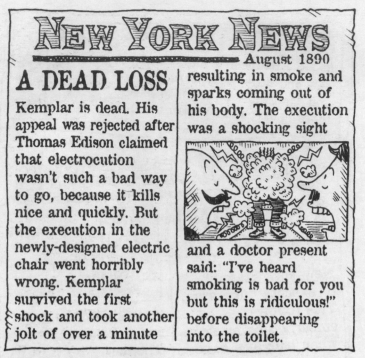

and a doctor present said: "I've heard smoking is bad for you but this is ridiculous!" before disappearing into the toilet.

WHAT HAPPENED NEXT?

Well, Westinghouse won. High voltage alternating current was the only way to move electricity any distance and in 1893 Westinghouse unveiled a powerful motor. It used alternating current and magnets that acted on first one side and then the other side of a metal loop. The motor was designed by a brilliant Croatian-born inventor named Nikola Tesla (1856–1943).

Some people thought Tesla was mad because he became a lonely old man who talked to the pigeons that lived in his New York apartment. Well, just imagine if one of the pigeon's had written Tesla's story. OK, I realize that's pretty unusual ... books by pigeons tend to be about flying.

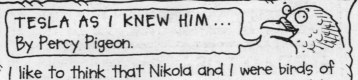

TESLA AS I KNEW HIM...
By Percy Pigeon.

I like to think that Nikola and I were birds of a feather and yeah, sure he told me about his life — he was no bird-brain, let me tell you!

Nikola was born in Croatia and his dad

N. TESLA

wanted him to be a priest but he wanted to be a scientist. So he talked his dad into letting him go to college. Mind you, he ruffled his teacher's feathers in a lesson on electric motors. Announced he could build a better electric motor — but no one believed him.

Anyway, Nikola was in a park when he got the idea for this motor. He was reading poetry (why wasn't he feeding the pigeons?) and he drew the design on the ground with a stick. He built the machine the next year and soon after he went to America to work for this Edison guy. Nikola went there with four cents in his pocket, some plans for a flying machine he never got round to building, and his electric motor.

ELECTRIC MOTOR

But things didn't work out. Edison didn't like alternating current (whatever that is) which is how Nikola's machine worked, and he didn't like Nikola either. So, Nikola got himself hired by Edison's rival Westinghouse. He dreamt up a new transformer for making high voltages (whatever that is) and

TRANSFORMER

Westinghouse marketed the machine. Old Nikola was an amazing guy. His lab was full of giant lightning flashes given out by his high-voltage alternating currents. I reckon he was looking for a flash of inspiration.

Yeah, people say Nikola got weird. But all he said was he was in touch with aliens and that he'd invented a death-ray to shoot down planes. Sounds sensible to me! I mean planes are a menace to high flying pigeons. Anyway Nikola was my idea of a nice guy — generous with the breadcrumbs and he didn't even blow a fuse when I got my aim wrong and pooed on his head.

Time was when the electric motor was the height of high technology. But those were the days when even your most ancient teachers were still running around with squeaky little voices and teddy bears. Today we have electric machines that, although still powered by electric motors, can do a lot more than simply go round and round. Machines that calculate sums and help you play really cool high-tech computer games. Machines stuffed full of wonderful, interesting electronics. Devices that control the flow of electricity and make it do useful work.

So if you want to do some useful work take a look at the next chapter ... it's AWESOME.

AWESOME ELECTRONICS

Electronics is really about one thing. Getting electrons in an electronic current to perform fancy tricks inside machines by the use of clever gadgets and circuits.

CLEVER CIRCUITS

What is a circuit? Well, for an electrical current to flow it's got to have somewhere to flow to. A circuit is simply a wire arranged in a circle for the current to flow along and on the way there might be switches and bulbs and various electrical gadgets. Here's your chance to test your teacher's knowledge of circuits.

TEACHER'S TEA-BREAK TEASER

You will need a bird. No, not a real pigeon like Percy – a toy bird will do. All you do is tap gently on the staffroom door. When it opens, smile innocently and ask:

HOW COME BIRDS CAN PERCH ON A HIGH-VOLTAGE WIRE AND NOT GET ELECTROCUTED?

Answer: If the bird's going to get a nasty shock the electricity must flow through its body. But electricity must have somewhere else to go before it can flow – as in a circuit. So if Percy isn't touching the ground or a pylon at the same time as touching the wire he's safe.

CRUCIAL CIRCUIT TRAINING

To discover more about circuits, let's imagine a unique fitness centre, and remember those sparky electron kids from the Atom Family? Well, now they're being put through their paces by fearsome fitness fanatic, A Tomm.

THE ELECTRON FIZZICAL TRAINING CAMP

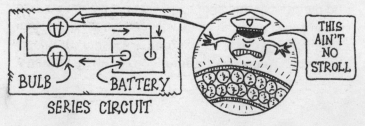

Crazy circuits

In our first event, the electrons race round a series of race tracks and light up bulbs and sound buzzers.

The first race is the series circuit – it's a nice, gentle warm up. The electrons must run from their battery hut round the wire, through the bulbs, and back to their battery. But so many electrons are crawling through the bulb wire that the rest get held up so they don't go too fast. A. Tomm isn't impressed.

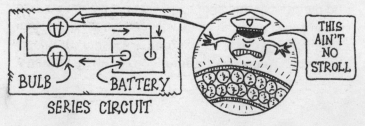

SERIES CIRCUIT

308

The second race is the parallel circuit. This is tougher and faster. A. Tomm has rearranged the wires so that there are two separate wires for each bulb. This means half the electrons can go one way and half can go the other so there's less of a bottleneck and the race is faster.

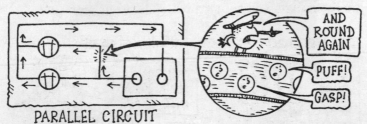

PARALLEL CIRCUIT

Super switches

Are you ready to make the switch? The electrons sure better be! In this exercise they'll have to get past the dreaded electrical switch. The switch is a springy piece of metal. When the switch is on the springy piece of metal is held down so the electrons crawling through the wire can crawl through it too. But they better be quick because when the switch is off the metal springs up and breaks the circuit. Leaving the electrons stranded!

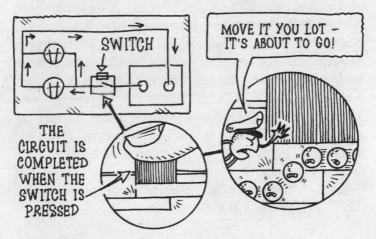

Fizzing fuses

Or should we call it frazzled fuses? In this heat (and boy, is it hot!) the electrons have to crawl though a narrow piece of wire. The resistance they get as they crawl through makes a lot of heat. If too many crawl in together the wire may melt so it's a real dangerous work-out.

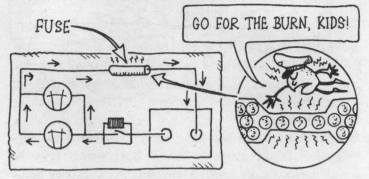

FUSE

GO FOR THE BURN, KIDS!

AND HERE ARE THE FULL FIZZICAL FACTS...

1 You get circuits everywhere electricity flows – so in your house a circuit runs round your light switches in each floor with separate circuits serving your power plugs. (Just imagine all those wires inside the walls!) As long as any of these switches is on, the current will flow. And that brings us to...

2 Switches. Besides power points you'll find switches in any electrical machine whether mains or battery operated. Well, how on Earth else are you going to turn it on – ask it nicely?

3 You get fuses in plugs and they're great for making sure too much current doesn't rush into an electrical machine. The number of amps in a fuse shows the amount of current it can take before it melts. Of course, if it did melt the machine wouldn't work and then you'd really blow a fuse!

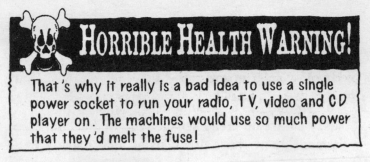

HORRIBLE HEALTH WARNING!

That's why it really is a bad idea to use a single power socket to run your radio, TV, video and CD player on. The machines would use so much power that they'd melt the fuse!

SUPER SEMI-CONDUCTORS

From the 1950s onwards electronics was revolutionized by the invention of the semiconductor by a team of scientists led by William Shockley (1910–1989) working at Bell Laboratories, USA. A semiconductor isn't anything to do with a semi-detached house, a semicolon or a semicircle. It's actually two slices of an element (type of atom) called silicon – you can imagine it as a slice of holey Swiss cheese on a slice of bread.

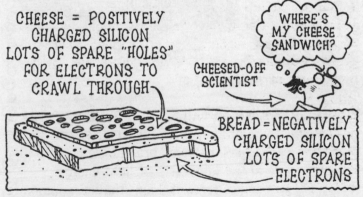

CHEESE = POSITIVELY CHARGED SILICON LOTS OF SPARE "HOLES" FOR ELECTRONS TO CRAWL THROUGH

WHERE'S MY CHEESE SANDWICH?

CHEESED-OFF SCIENTIST

BREAD = NEGATIVELY CHARGED SILICON LOTS OF SPARE ELECTRONS

The electrons are quite happy crawling from the bread to the cheese but they can't return from the cheese to the bread. This means you can use a semi-conductor to control the direction that electrons flow. And then they can even be used to make power from the sun!

Shocking electricity fact file

NAME: Solar power

THE BASIC FACTS: A solar cell is simply that tasty cheese on bread semiconductor. Sunlight is made up of those tiny blips of light called photons.

1 Photons knock electrons in the bread free of their atoms.

2 Free electrons go off to explore the cheese.

3 More electrons move from the bread to take their place. This makes an electric current.

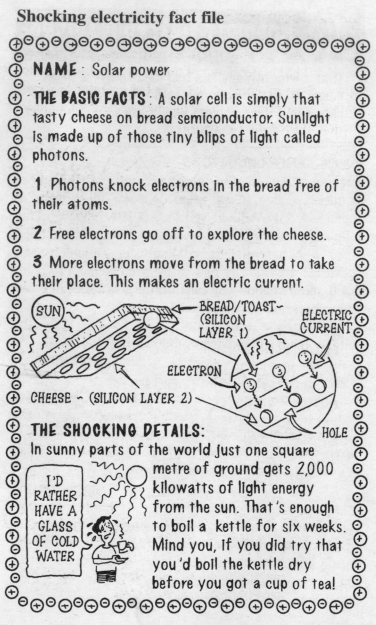

SUN

BREAD/TOAST ~ (SILICON LAYER 1)

ELECTRIC CURRENT

ELECTRON

CHEESE ~ (SILICON LAYER 2)

HOLE

THE SHOCKING DETAILS:
In sunny parts of the world just one square metre of ground gets 2,000 kilowatts of light energy from the sun. That's enough to boil a kettle for six weeks. Mind you, if you did try that you'd boil the kettle dry before you got a cup of tea!

I'D RATHER HAVE A GLASS OF COLD WATER

SUPER SOLAR POWER

Amongst the uses found for solar power are a way to make power for spacecraft, experimental cars that can travel at 112 km per hour (70 miles per hour), and a solar-powered hat invented in 1967 by US inventor W Dahly. It used solar power to drive an electric fan hidden inside the hat to keep the wearer's head cool.

Sadly the invention proved a flop. I guess it didn't have too many fans.

Now back to semiconductors – did you know that without them a computer wouldn't work?

SUPER SILICON CHIPS

No, this is nothing to do with French fries. The chip is a semiconductor found in computers and many other gadgets. On its surface are hundreds and thousands of tiny switches called transistors. Each transistor is like a set of traffic lights at a road junction.

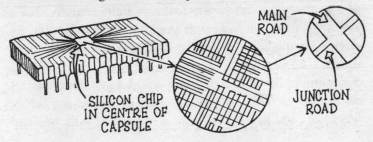

SILICON CHIP IN CENTRE OF CAPSULE

MAIN ROAD

JUNCTION ROAD

Electrons can only go along the "main road" if the current is also flowing for the "junction" road. By switching this "junction" current on and off very fast the transistor makes a current of one-off electrical pulses on the "main road" that make up basic computer code.

SILICON SECRETS

1 A silicon chip is made of silicon. (So how come you knew that already?) Anyway you can find silicon in sand. Yes, it's true, the insides of your computer probably started off loafing about on a beach somewhere.

2 Chips are shrinking. At the end of the 1960s the smallest silicon chip was 200,000 atoms across. By the end of the 1970s the smallest chip was 10,000 atoms across and by the end of the 1980s they were ten times smaller. And yet the finished chip is as complicated in its plan as a large city.

...3 BILLION DOLLARS TO DEVELOP THIS TINY CHIP, CARTER...AND YOU JUST DROPPED IT!!!!

Incredibly, it's now possible to make a chip a few dozen atoms across ... and in the future? Well, actually that's about as far as you can go. If you made a chip smaller its circuits would have corners too tight for electrons to flow round.

3 You might be wondering how you can get all that detail on a chip too tiny to hold. Actually, the boring fiddly work of adding the different types of silicon and aluminium to carry the current is done by robots. The only thing we humans need to worry about is getting dust or dandruff or dried snot in the chips and ruining them. (Of course robots don't have this problem.)

4 Nowadays silicon chips are found in loads of machines and not just computers. You can find silicon chips controlling DVD players and Play Stations, and Andy Mann's mobile phone and even walking, talking, peeing dolls. Yes – it really is chips with everything!

MIND YOU, IT STOPPED WORKING WHEN I DROPPED SALT AND VINEGAR ON IT!

There's a gap of 2,600 years between old Thales rubbing a lump of amber with a bit of fur to the latest up-to-the -minute silicon chips. Although it's a long time the vast leaps forward in technology are even more astonishing. But where's the tide of technology taking us? Are we heading for an electronic wonderland or could we slip back to the dark ages? What kind of shocks await us?

Better read on and find out...

THE FUTURE

EPILOGUE: A SHOCKING FUTURE?

In the olden days before electricity life was hard and cold and comfortless and slow. But that was then and today the world of electricity and electronics is buzzing with new ideas.

Some ideas are exciting, some are important and some are rather silly. Which ones do you think will take root, and which will quietly disappear like the solar-powered hat and the wobbling toilet seat? And what will they think of next? Let's switch on the TV.

TOMORROW TODAY

Welcome to Tomorrow Today the TV programme that tells you about tomorrow's technology today.

And now over to Japan where scientists have invented a robot cat.

Battery-powered motors enable the cat to blink, rub its eyes and jump. Touch sensors make it purr when stroked and it can also spit and snarl. In fact, the only thing it can't do is catch mice!

And pee on the carpet?

Researchers from IBM have created a computer screen that gives you a picture as good as the very best TV. It works like the display of a calculator which uses liquid crystal blocks that give out light when an electric current runs across them.

The screen has no fewer than 5.5 million pixels (dots of light) powered by 15.7 transistors and 4.21 km of wiring.

Gosh!

That's nothing. A British university Professor has had a silicon chip-based control device implanted into his arm. The gadget switches on lights and computers without the professor having to touch them!

Any volunteers for this op?

And finally you can relax and unwind with a TV box. This nifty device turns a laptop computer into a TV and video recorder with full video editing facilities.

Besides new gadgets, scientists are working on longer-term research which might in time lead to new technology and more new gadgets. So what does the future hold? We've asked Tiddles the robot cat (alias Mystic Mog) to gaze into her mysteriously cloudy bowl of milk. Here's what she saw...

1 It's life ... but not as we know it
In 1952 Stanley Miller at the University of Chicago fired an electric spark through a mixture of gases. He was trying to copy the effect of lightning on gases in the air thousands of millions of years ago. His experiment had a remarkable result: amino acids – complex chemicals found in living things – formed from the gases. Scientists are still looking at ways in which electricity in the form of lightning may have given rise to life on Earth.
Prediction 1
Scientists find out how to make a new kind of life-form in a test tube using electricity and chemicals.

2 Powering ahead

Scientists in different parts of the world are developing plans to use the power of tides to make electricity. Although their plans vary they all depend on using the water rushing through narrow channels to drive turbines. In the 2000s other scientists were looking at building a huge chimney in the South African desert. Warmed by the hot sun, air will rise up the chimney and power generators to make electricity.

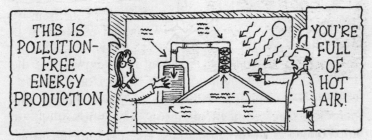

Prediction 2

One of these plans will come off and create a new technology which can make electricity for nothing *for ever.*

3 Real cool power

As long ago as 1911 Dutch scientist Heike Kamerliingh-Onnes (1853–1926) found that at very low temperatures, say just above -273°C (-459°F) metals like the mercury in a thermometer become superconductors. This means they lose their resistance to electricity – isn't that super! In 1957 a team led by US scientist John Bardeen (1908–1991) calculated that superconductor atoms wobble less when they are very cold allowing electrons to swim between the atoms without being knocked off course.

319

Prediction 3

Scientists invent a substance that allows electricity to run through it easily at room temperature. This opens the door to a new generation of electric machines that need scarcely any power to run.

Despite the promise of future progress most people still find electricity mysterious, but hopefully having read this book you won't be one of them. All most people know is that electricity is terribly useful and sometimes shockingly dangerous. But of course, electricity is much, much more.

Electricity is amazing. Amazing in its power and the limitless variety of the tasks that it can perform. And it's totally gobsmacking to think that the power behind this incredible force comes from astonishing blips of energy and matter – electrons and atoms. Yep, the same electrons and atoms that help a pelican find its way home and make your heart beat and give shape and substance to everything in the universe. Including you.

And that's the SHOCKING TRUTH!

SEE YA!

SHOCKING ELECTRICITY

QUIZ

Now find out if you're a
Shocking Electricity expert!

Electrical impulses are everywhere. In the Earth, in the clouds – even in your horrible science teacher. Without electricity there'd be no light bulbs, no television, nothing fun at all. Take these quick quizzes to see how much you really know about this fatal force...

Astonishing electrons

If your brain is fully switched on by this book, you'll know by now that electricity is made of electrons – tiny blips that spend their lives whizzing around the nucleus of atoms. But what do you really know about these powerful particles and their amazing effects?

1 What charge does an electron have?
a) Positive
b) Negative
c) Dangerous

WHY DO I FEEL SO NEGATIVE?

2 What is the name of the particle given out by electrons as they lose energy and slow down?
a) Pooton
b) Proton
c) Photon

3 What is static electricity?
a) A form of electricity in which the electrons stop moving completely.
b) A form of electricity in which electrons are transferred from one thing to another, changing the electrical charge of each.

c) A form of electricity that looks all fuzzy through a microscope.

4 How can you rearrange the atoms in a magnet so that it doesn't work any more?
a) By frying it over a strong heat.
b) By drowning it in salty water.
c) By slicing it in half with a chainsaw.

5 How do batteries make an electric current?
a) By removing all the positive charges from the metal casing.
b) By mixing two chemicals together.
c) By squashing together lots of tiny magnets.

6 What happens when you hold an electrified object?
a) Your muscles squeeze together so you can't let go and you'll probably die a horrible death.
b) It interrupts the electrical impulses in the heart and you'll probably die a horrible death.
c) The electricity fries your brain and you'll definitely die a horrible death.

7 Where is the safest place to shelter during an electric storm?
a) In a car.
b) Under a tree.
c) Under an umbrella.

8 How fast can electrons move?
a) About the speed of sound.
b) About the speed of a horse.
c) About the speed of light.

Answers:
1b; 2c; 3b; 4a; 5b; 6a; 7a; 8c

Horrible electricity facts

*Electricity flows all around us (as well as inside us),
but it took scientists a long time to get to grips with it,
and along the way they made some messy mistakes.
Below are some silly statements about electricity – can
you figure out if these fascinating force facts are true or
false?*

1 Electricity flows from positively charged areas to
negatively charged areas.
2 You can make electricity from farts.
3 Animals like sharks and bees can detect electrical
pulses in humans.
4 Electricity always finds the quickest route to the ground.
5 Electricity can travel through metal wires.
6 Electric shocks aren't always bad – they can be used to
re-start the heart if it stops beating.
7 The Earth is just one great big magnet.
8 The human body contains enough electricity to light
the fairy lights on a Christmas tree.

Answers:

1 False. It's the other way around (although brilliant Ben Franklin got this wrong too...).

2 True. Farts contain the gas methane, which can power generators.

3 True. And it can make them pretty angry!

4 True. Which is why it's not a good idea to stand under an umbrella in a lightning storm – the metal in the umbrella will attract the electricity and channel is straight to the ground – through you!

5 False. Ha ha. Trick question – in fact, electricity travels through a field around the wire.

6 True. Doctors use a shockingly clever machine called a defibrillator that passes an electric current into the heart to restart it.

7 True. The Earth's core is surrounded by a massive sea of melted metal that sends out electric and magnetic forces.

8 True. But don't worry – if you weren't a bundle of electric pulses you'd be, well, dead.

Strange scientists

They say it takes all sorts, but the silly scientists who helped us understand electricity were some of the strangest ever. Experiments with electricity can be horribly dangerous, and some of these fantastic physicists diced with death. Just take this quiz and find out for yourself...

1 What natural force did barmy Benjamin Franklin investigate in his most famous experiment? (Clue: It was certainly enlightening.)

2 What did John Joseph Thomson use to bend the ray of electrons in his cathode ray tube experiment? (Clue: It was an attractive experiment.)

3 What kind of electricity did ancient Greek Thales of Miletus experiment with? (Clue: It was certainly hair-raising.)

4 What amazing invention did Robert Van de Graf come up with? (Clue: It generated some interest at the time.)

5 What happened when Luigi Galvani attached his dead pet frog to the iron bars on his windows? (Clue: It made the silly scientist jump!)

I'D BETTER READ ON...

6 What substance did Alessandro Volta find to be the best conductor for passing an electric current between two pieces of metal? (Clue: Water surprise!)

7 What magnetic mystery did William Gilbert solve while playing around with his compass? (Clue: He remained well-grounded despite his discovery.)

8 What magnificent machine did mad Michael Faraday build? (Clue: He was driven to it.)

Answers:
1 Lightning.
2 A magnet.
3 Static electricity.
4 An electrical generator.
5 The frog's legs jumped around as if it was still alive.
6 Salt water.
7 That the Earth is magnetic.
8 The electric motor.

Mysterious measurements

There are all sorts of ways of measuring electricity and most of the units of measurement are named after the strange scientists who discovered them. You've met some of them in this book, so now see if you can match the mad measurement with its meaning.

1 Amp
2 Volt
3 Watt
4 Ohm
5 Farad
6 Watthour
7 Coulomb
8 Henry

a) A measure of electrical resistance.
b) A measure of electrical storage capacity.
c) A measure of electric current.
d) A measure of electrical energy.
e) A measure of reaction to changes in the magnetic field.
f) A measure of electrical pressure.
g) A measure of electrical charge.
h) A measure of electrical power.

Answers:
1c; 2f; 3h; 4a; 5b; 6d; 7g; 8e

HORRIBLE INDEX

330

331

Nick Arnold has been writing stories and books since he was a youngster, but never dreamt he'd find fame writing about Horrible Science. His research involved building his own steam engine and swimming with an electric eel and he enjoyed every minute of it.

When he's not delving into Horrible Science, he spends his spare time eating pizza, riding his bike and thinking up corny jokes (though not all at the same time).

Tony De Saulles picked up his crayons when he was still in nappies and has been doodling ever since. He takes Horrible Science very seriously and even agreed to sketch radioactive atoms and test how electricity runs through lightning. Fortunately, he has made a full recovery.

When he's not out with his sketchpad, Tony likes to write poetry and play squash, though he hasn't written any poetry about squash yet.

ISBN 978 0439 94447 2

ISBN 978 0439 94450 2